I0605633

Make It Plant-Based!
Filipino

Make It Plant-Based!

Filipino

60+ RECIPES FOR VEGAN SOUPS, STEWS, NOODLES, SNACKS, AND DESSERTS

Ria Elciario-McKeown

Mehreen Karim, series editor
Photographs by Emma Fishman

WORKMAN PUBLISHING • NEW YORK

Workman
Workman Publishing
Hachette Book Group, Inc.
1290 Avenue of the Americas
New York, NY 10104
workman.com

Workman is an imprint of Workman Publishing, a division of Hachette Book Group, Inc. The Workman name and logo are registered trademarks of Hachette Book Group, Inc.

Design by Suet Chong
Cover illustration by str33t cat/Shutterstock, Inc.

Library of Congress Cataloging-in-Publication Data is available.

ISBN 978-1-5235-2562-1

First Edition May 2025

Printed in China on responsibly sourced paper.

10 9 8 7 6 5 4 3 2 1

In loving memory of
Diana Cerise Calma
and
Andiolina Dalisay Salaver

Contents

Preface

Growing up, vegetables were never at the center of my mom's cooking. My family, like most Filipino families, often ate meat-heavy meals and never had a reason to change that. But as I grew older and met people whose dietary regimens differed from mine, I redefined my cooking with an appreciation for plant-based ingredients and how delicious they taste in Filipino recipes.

I spent most of my childhood waking up to the scent of garlic emanating from my mom's sinangag (garlic fried rice), which she often made from the previous night's leftover rice. On Sunday mornings, the smell of simmering lugaw (congee or rice porridge) with boiled eggs and tuyo (fried sun-dried fish) lingered until breakfast was over. At one point, guessing the scent of what was coming from the kitchen became a game, and my curiosity eventually led me to observe in admiration while my mom and lola (grandmother) cooked and conjured mouth-watering aromas.

I sat in the kitchen, fascinated by the way they cooked without following a recipe. They threw bay leaves and whole garlic cloves into pots, moved ever so swiftly as they retrieved seasonings from the cupboard, and stood by the stovetop, examining the magic they were making. A timer didn't exist in our kitchen because they knew exactly when a dish was ready just by using their intuition. It was spellbinding, and I wanted to be able to do it, too. If I was patient, they'd allow me to help out with small but mighty tasks like peeling vegetables or shredding cheese. And in return for my hard work, they'd teach me how to cook. As I practiced the foundations of simple techniques, I fell in love with Filipino cooking.

Eating and cooking Filipino food was my way of staying connected to my heritage after my parents and I moved from Manila to Toronto. My mom continued to cook the Filipino dishes I loved, replacing native Filipino produce with whatever was accessible to us.

If she couldn't find kangkong (water spinach), she'd use regular leaf spinach, or sometimes even opt for a hearty leafy vegetable like kale. Vegetables have always been a part of Filipino cuisine, but I didn't realize until later in life that they were more than just an accessory to meat-centric dishes. My mom's quickness to adapt to a new selection of produce and Western ingredients inspired me to become flexible in how I cook Filipino food, too.

When I met my husband, who is completely vegetarian, many years later, the concept of having a plant-forward diet was foreign to me. When I attempted to show him Filipino food around Toronto, the only options he had to eat were lumpiang gulay (vegetable spring rolls)—if he was lucky—and rice. I was determined to make him fall in love with Filipino food the way I did, so I reimagined the dishes I loved growing up and taught myself to employ plant-based ingredients as the foundation of my cooking. After studying various cooking concepts at home and in culinary school, I began to test different ways to make plant-forward products the star of every meal while making sure the flavors I knew and loved remained the same. I started actively searching for new ingredients at grocery stores and discovered a wide array of vegan products that I started to incorporate into my cooking. It made me realize I didn't always need to reach for animal-derived ingredients to cook something that was both nourishing and delicious. I learned to transform mushrooms—a vegetable I used to loathe—into a saucy, umami-packed dish to eat with rice, my favorite sweet and sour sauce, and banana ketchup. I started layering soy sauces and vinegar, and pairing the textures of tender vegetables with crispy toppings—all in order to develop recipes that transport me to the kitchen where I first learned to cook with confidence and intuition. On every page of this book, I share and celebrate my plant-based Filipino discoveries.

Ria Elciario-McKeown

Introduction

Before fusion food became a part of our common lexicon, Filipinos already had a long history of merging cultures and cuisines via culinary techniques. We approached cooking as an instrument to stay true to our roots while learning new ways of living during colonial eras in the Philippines.

Our food primarily relies on a mix of sweet, salty, and sour notes—what I like to call the trifecta of Filipino flavors. They are thoughtfully layered in our food, complementing each other in every bite. With a handful of pantry staples such as brown sugar, soy sauce, and cane vinegar, you'll learn how to cook a harmonious, plant-based dish that packs a punch and leaves you craving your next bite.

Adobo, the most popular dish in Filipino cuisine—the culinary headliner, if you will—perfectly represents both the history of Filipino food and its signature trifecta of sweet, salty, and sour flavors. The evolution of adobo, a saucy, meat-based dish, symbolizes just how much our ancestors intermingled diverse cuisines while honoring our culture. Marinated in an umami-packed concoction of vinegar, soy sauce, brown sugar, and aromatics, every ingredient symbolizes a time and place in Filipino history. Despite the word "adobo" coming from Spain, the concept already existed in the Philippines. Long before Spainiards arrived in 1521 and conquered in 1565, Filipinos preserved proteins using salt and vinegar to adapt to the tropical climate. The foreign name "adobo" stuck to the dish in spite of its native origin, likely in reaction to the complexity of our cultural diversity: Filipinos consist of 182 ethnolinguistic groups that use different dialects. Later, through extensive trading with our Chinese neighbors, we were introduced to soy sauce, and the adobo we know and love was more or less complete. Today every region and family has their own version of this signature dish, and it no longer requires meat. Instead, you can use different vegetables such as mushrooms, green beans, and eggplant to make a delicious adobo.

No matter how you make your adobo, one thing for sure is that it will come with rice. Since its arrival in 3000 BCE, we have cultivated rice in various parts of the Philippine archipelago and made it a part of our day-to-day cuisine. As you explore the recipes in this book, you'll discover that Filipinos eat it for breakfast, lunch, dinner—and even dessert. No ulam (side dish) is complete without kanin (rice). It's what separates a meal from a snack. It's what makes a meal *a meal*. In a way, the evolution of adobo and our use of rice represent how Filipinos learned to adopt foreign ingredients and make them our own.

While this book is about plant-based cooking, it's important to acknowledge the significant influence that meat has played in shaping the way we cook and eat today. In ancient Filipino traditions, animal sacrifices like roasting a whole pig were a common practice during festive thanksgiving celebrations. The arrival of Spaniards and Americans further shaped the role of meat in Filipino cooking when they introduced us to ham and fried chicken. Meat stars in most traditional Filipino stir-fries, stews, and street food, and no part of the animal ever goes to waste. In many ways, Filipinos learned to be frugal in cooking throughout our centuries of colonial subjugation and trade. Take, for example, sisig, a popular sizzling dish. Its origins are found in using excess meats, such as offal and jowls, obtained from the commissaries of American military facilities in Pampanga. Locals purchased the unwanted meats for cheap, boiled them, and tossed them in a tangy vinegar dressing, creating the earliest version of sisig. The dish evolved in the 1970s when Aling Lucing of Pampanga accidentally burned an order of barbecued pig's ears at her eatery. Instead of discarding them and starting over, she chopped them up, tossed them in the same vinegar dressing, and presented them to her customer as her new sisig.

Plant-based Filipino recipes follow in the Philippines' history of resourcefulness. Using an array of fresh produce and shelf stable pantry items, these recipes will teach you how to wring the most flavor and food out of your ingredients in the name of sustainable cooking and becoming a smarter, more strategic home cook.

Once you learn to transition animal products out of your cooking, you'll discover that plant-based versions of Filipino classics remain as delicious as their origins. Coconut milk, a popular plant-based milk, is already used in many traditional Filipino stews and desserts. By homing in on vegetables, harnessing their intrinsic flavors, and making them the star of the plate, even the simplest of dishes are elevated. Reimagining the use of common vegetables allows beginner cooks to build a strong foundation of skills such as cutting techniques and become familiar with standard cooking times. From washing, chopping, and storing to different ways of cooking, learning to master plant-based ingredients will actually help you save time in the kitchen.

The more you cook with fresh produce, the more you'll appreciate the beauty of shopping with the seasons. You'll understand that tomatoes at their summer peak are juiciest. Cabbage and root vegetables shine in the colder months. And ripe carabao and ataulfo mangoes are their sweetest in late spring. By going with the flow of the seasons and having a well-stocked pantry, you can create delicious recipes all year round. In this book, you'll find a range of recipes that cater to every season, as well as every home cook, no matter your level of expertise. From quick and easy stovetop dinners to work-from-home lunches to traditional celebratory foods, you'll discover that great cooking is not about complex seasonings or expensive ingredients, but rather about balancing flavors and textures.

In Sizzling Mushroom and Tofu Sisig (page 101), you'll combine chewy mushrooms with crispy tofu for a mouthwatering bite. When you make Vegetable Noodle Soup (page 69), adding toasted sesame oil not only enhances the dish's richness but also adds a delicate, nutty flavor. Squash and Green Bean–Coconut Stew (page 57) calls for custardy cubes of kabocha squash and gets topped with crispy tofu. Reimagining Filipino classics into exciting plant-based dishes will show you just how fun and liberating it is to cook creatively with whatever you have on hand.

Despite my love for the classic dishes that shaped my culinary style today, some of my favorite recipes are the ones that deviate from tradition in order to utilize accessible, plant-based ingredients. Take the Roasted Mushrooms with Sticky Adobo Sauce (page 95) with a mouth-puckering tangy glaze drizzled over top—this combination stays true to the classic flavors of adobo while dressing up the humble mushroom to become the star of the dinner table, not to mention of the dish.

Most recipes are written to be customizable so that your cooking experience is as convenient as it is delicious. Throughout you will find instructions on how to easily source specialty Filipino ingredients, but most recipes also suggest substitutions for items that may be less accessible to you. You'll learn to embrace canned foods and shelf stable ingredients the way Filipinos incorporate them into everyday cooking—using what's available without compromising on flavor. Look out for Freestyle It boxes, which contain notes on how you can improvise and substitute certain ingredients, and Meal-ify It boxes, which lend suggestions on making a proper meal out of a side dish. As you come across new Filipino dishes in this book, think of the recipes as mini crash courses on fundamental Filipino cooking techniques. They may feel unfamiliar at first, but after cooking even just one or two recipes, you'll find your flow in the versatile nature of Filipino cooking—all while celebrating the Philippines' rich food history. I hope each recipe will leave you with a newfound appreciation for the symphony of flavors that is Filipino cuisine.

Keep Your Kitchen Stocked

Whether you're a beginner or an experienced home cook, a well-stocked kitchen is crucial to your success. Many of these essential ingredients are used frequently because they add uniquely Filipino flavors and textures to dishes. Stocking your pantry with a diverse array of ingredients will allow you to create a wide range of dishes without having to run to the store every time you want to cook.

PANTRY

RICE

Rice is an incredibly versatile ingredient that can be used in a variety of Filipino dishes, both sweet and savory. Pair any white rice, preferably jasmine or Calrose, with stews, stir-fries, and other side dishes as it tends to be soft and absorb flavors easily, making it an excellent base for many dishes. Glutinous rice is perfect for creating delicious traditional dishes and desserts; it has a higher starch content and is stickier than other types of rice, making it ideal for recipes that require a chewier texture.

SOY SAUCE

Soy sauce, the deeply flavored, salty liquid condiment most commonly associated with Japanese and Chinese dishes, is an integral ingredient in almost every Filipino meal. Whether you're cooking a stir-fry or noodles, or making a quick dipping sauce, its unique umami and savoriness deepens any dish's flavors with just a few drops. There are various brands of soy sauces you can buy, but try to look for Filipino brands such as Datu Puti, Marca Piña, or Silver Swan for best results.

CANNED COCONUT MILK AND CREAM

Coconuts play a significant role in Filipino cuisine and are essential in many traditional dishes. They are a versatile ingredient that adds a uniquely nutty flavor and creamy texture to a variety of dishes. When buying coconut milk or cream, it's important to read the labels carefully. Coconut milk is a lot runnier than coconut cream, which has a thick consistency. Using the wrong one can significantly affect the outcome of your dish. They are not interchangeable since they can result in a dish that's too thin or too thick and may lack the flavor and texture you're looking for. Seek out Aroy-D and Grace brands, which are usually easy to find.

SESAME OIL

Sesame oil is not a common ingredient in Filipino cuisine, but its distinctly nutty fragrance and taste imbue plant-based dishes with a toasty flavor. When used sparingly, just a few drops add an earthy yet savory taste to any dish. Opt for toasted sesame oil—it's made from toasted sesame seeds, guaranteeing a more deeply flavored oil.

BROWN SUGAR

Once you start treating brown sugar as a seasoning instead of an occasional dessert ingredient, you will learn how to develop complex flavors in your cooking. You can use brown sugar in savory stir-fries and stews, paired with lots of garlic and soy sauce. While learning to season as you go, lean on brown sugar to balance anything that tastes too salty or acidic.

CANE VINEGAR

Compared to other popular types such as rice vinegar, this slightly sweeter version rounds out its acidity without tasting too saccharine. Made from fermented sugarcane juice, it boasts a complex, tart flavor that helps bring out the sweetness of vegetables and balances any savory dish. You can find a variety of brands in Asian supermarkets sitting near the soy sauces. Seek out Filipino brands like Datu Puti, Marca Piña, or Silver Swan, which usually come in 1 liter bottles.

DRIED BAY LEAVES

Dried bay leaves add a subtle earthiness to soups and sauces. They're essential to traditional recipes like adobo that you'll come across frequently in this book. You can easily find dried bay leaves in the spice section of your grocery store, packaged in either a plastic bag or jar. Use dried bay leaves, because fresh bay leaves can dominate the other flavors in a dish if left in the pot for too long.

POTATO STARCH

Cornstarch is indispensable for thickening certain dishes, but potato starch is your best friend when it comes to frying. Potato starch cooks fast just like cornstarch, so whatever you coat it with crisps up quickly. However, since potatoes generally have more starch than corn, potato starch tends to be stickier, which results in a crispy, chewy crust—owed to the residual heat that slowly continues to cook the interior of the coating after it's been removed from the oil. You will find it at any Asian supermarket such as H Mart or Seafood City in some parts of the US and Canada, or even local grocery stores that sell Bob's Red Mill products—but any brand will do. To make things easier in the kitchen, transfer it to an airtight jar or deli container so you don't have to fuss with the plastic bag each time.

SWEET CHILI SAUCE

Sweet chili sauce and crispy vegetable spring rolls are an unbeaten combination. Each drop of sauce provides a tangy kick from its vinegar, but is rounded out by a dominant sweetness that perfectly complements salty fried foods. Whether drizzled, dipped, or used as a glaze, sweet chili sauce brings a Filipino flair to the table. You can easily find Thai sweet chili sauce at almost any grocery store, but if you shop in an Asian supermarket you'll be able to buy Filipino brands like UFC and Jufran.

CHILI CRISP

Adding chili crisp to any savory meal is an excellent way to elevate the simplest of dishes with added texture and delicate spice. Even a small drizzle of this versatile condiment provides a burst of heat and a satisfying crunch to stir-fries, soups, rice, and more. Nowadays, you can find chili crisp at large grocery stores without a hitch, but my tried-and-true favorite is Lao Gan Ma, which is easy to source at Asian supermarkets.

BANANA KETCHUP

Banana ketchup is a must-have condiment in Filipino households. Its sweetness comes from a mixture of bananas and brown sugar, which complements the deep umami notes in tomatoes. Unlike its classic American counterpart, banana ketchup is less tart and slightly spicier. It doesn't have any hint of banana flavor despite its name. Use it as a dipping sauce as you would any regular ketchup, or as a seasoning for fried rice to add a hint of sweetness. I like UFC and Jufran (which calls it "banana sauce"), which you can find in most Asian supermarkets.

ANNATTO POWDER

Annatto powder comes from the seeds of the achiote tree (*Bixa orellana*), often referred to as the "lipstick tree" due to its striking red color. It's a vibrant and aromatic spice created by grinding the seeds of the annatto plant. When sprinkled on sauces or soups, annatto provides a warm and slightly peppery flavor to Filipino dishes, much like paprika. You can find annatto (also called achuete or achiote powder) in the spice section of any Asian supermarket or even Costco. I like to use Mama Sita's and Goya.

FRIDGE & FREEZER

EXTRA FIRM TOFU

Tofu, the soy-based protein powerhouse we know and love, absorbs any flavor you apply to it, making it a popular choice for plant-based eaters looking for a nutritious and delicious centerpiece for any meal. When purchasing tofu, opt for extra firm since it contains less water and crisps up faster when cooked. The less moisture in the tofu, the quicker and easier it is to use in these recipes. To press any excess moisture from your tofu, simply wrap it in a couple of paper towels and gently squeeze the tofu over the sink. Once the tofu is dry, it can be sliced, diced, or crumbled and added to a variety of dishes such as stir-fries, salads, and soups.

SPRING ROLL WRAPPERS

When it comes to making shatteringly crispy spring rolls, having the right type of wrapper is of the utmost importance. When fried, they turn crispy and golden brown, providing the perfect contrast to soft or chewy fillings. You can find them at any Asian supermarket. Remember to check the label carefully, since these wrappers tend to be in the same section as wonton or egg roll wrappers, which may look similar but taste different.

BANANA LEAVES

Banana leaves are used to wrap rice cakes and to serve food on directly (see The Kamayan Way on page 141). The leaves are large and fragrant, imparting a delicate and sweet grassiness to all foods they touch. Cut the leaves to whatever size works best for the occasion and lay them flat on your dinner table to put the food directly on top, as you would with a grazing board. You can find banana leaves in your local Asian or Latin American grocery store packaged next to fresh produce or in the freezer section. Use as many as you need and store the rest in your freezer for future recipes.

Breakfast & Brunch

From warm bowls of savory porridge to sweet and creamy smoothies, Filipino breakfast offers a little something for everyone to kick-start the day.

Mango and Coconut Chia Pudding

In this variation on mango sticky rice, instead of cooking rice you stir chia seeds and coconut milk together and refrigerate the mixture overnight until it doubles in size and turns into a pudding. The pairing of sweet and tangy mango and creamy coconut tastes just as divine in chia pudding form. This recipe is an efficient make-ahead breakfast for anyone with a sweet tooth, and it's also a nutrient-packed snack.

SERVES 4 TO 6

1 can (400 ml) coconut milk

½ cup (95 g) chia seeds

3 tablespoons maple syrup, plus more if needed

1 teaspoon pure vanilla extract

Pinch of kosher salt

2 ripe yellow mangoes, such as Carabao or Ataúlfo

Black sesame seeds, for garnish

Combine the coconut milk, chia seeds, maple syrup, vanilla, and salt in a large mixing bowl. Stir until fully combined. Transfer the pudding to an airtight container and store it in the refrigerator for at least 3 hours or overnight.

Cut off the mango cheeks by standing each mango on end and slicing straight down along the seed. Lay each cheek skin side down on a cutting board and carefully scoop the fruit out using a large spoon, making sure to keep the whole cheek intact. Place the flat side down on the cutting board and cube the mango cheek into bite-sized chunks.

Assemble the pudding by scooping a few tablespoons into each serving bowl. Place a few mango chunks on top and sprinkle on some black sesame seeds.

Store leftovers in the refrigerator for up to 1 week.

Breakfast Chocolate Porridge

CHAMPORADO

A true breakfast of champions involves just a little chocolate. If you have a sweet tooth in the morning, this warm bowl of rich cocoa-infused porridge is for you. This recipe takes close to an hour to prepare, so make it for a leisurely weekend breakfast, or ahead of time for an easy reheatable breakfast.

SERVES 4 TO 6

- 1 cup (195 g) glutinous rice
- 1 can (400 ml) coconut milk
- 2 cups (400 ml) water
- ½ cup (40 g) unsweetened cocoa powder
- ½ cup (110 g) packed dark brown sugar, plus more if needed
- Pinch of kosher salt
- 1 tablespoon coconut cream (optional)
- Pinch of flaky sea salt (optional)

Rinse the rice two or three times in a fine-mesh strainer under cold water until the water runs clear.

Warm a saucepan over medium-low heat for 2 minutes, then add the coconut milk, water, cocoa powder, and brown sugar. Whisk to combine and simmer for 3 to 4 minutes, until the sugars dissolve. Add the rice and salt and stir to combine. Cover the pot and simmer for 40 minutes, stirring every 10 to 12 minutes to prevent the rice from sticking to the bottom of the pot, until thick and creamy. Remove from heat, taste, and add more sugar as desired.

Serve in bowls, with a drizzle of coconut cream for extra creaminess and a sprinkle of flaky sea salt to balance the sweetness if you like.

If making ahead, store the cooled champorado in an airtight container in the refrigerator for up to 3 days. Reheat in the microwave with 1 tablespoon water since it might thicken in the refrigerator.

The Cultural Significance of Rice in Filipino Cuisine

Around 3000 BCE, Austronesian peoples brought rice to the Philippines. Since then, this crop has sailed across the archipelago's 7,641 islands, with all regions adapting it to their cooking and cultural traditions.

Rice started out as a special grain for the upper class. Some Indigenous Filipinos harvested it for religious rituals and shared it with their respective communities because they believed spirits lived inside the grains. But it wasn't widely considered a staple ingredient due to the intense maintenance required to cultivate and grow the crop. When the Spanish colonizers arrived in the Philippines, they introduced the technique of farming by using carabaos (water buffalos), which led to an increase in rice production. The Indigenous rituals were eventually dismissed as superstitions, but rice remained an ingredient available only to the elites.

Centuries later, during World War II, the Japanese army killed nearly 70 percent of the carabaos, preventing farmers from growing rice. Once World War II was over, the government introduced a campaign called the Green Revolution and established the International Rice Research Institute (IRRI) to help reduce poverty and hunger. Rice farmers began to incorporate fertilizers and other farming techniques that skyrocketed rice production and shifted the way Filipinos ate.

Over the years, Filipinos continued to increase the use of rice as the foundation of their cuisine. Whether in soups, snacks, main dishes, or baked goods—you name it—rice can do it. Rice remains the background of every Filipino's ulam (side dishes), and can be found in delicacies across different regions. You can even purchase rice from fast-food chains like McDonald's and Jollibee, served with dishes like lumpia and longganisa.

One of the country's proudest sights is the rice terraces of the Philippine Cordilleras, which were hand-carved by the people of Ifugao and created beautiful emerald-green mountains about 5,000 feet (1,500 meters) above sea level. The terraces and the ancient method of farming can be traced as far back as the precolonial era about 2,000 years ago and have been passed down from generation to generation. These terraces continue to be a source of rice for various communities living in the Cordilleras.

Today, rice remains at the heart of every Filipino's table, regardless of socioeconomic status or where they live in the world. It is a part of the Filipino identity, and the food that reminds us all of home.

Cozy Rice Porridge

LUGAW

This ultra comforting rice porridge is similar to congee, but with an added peppery and smoky flavor thanks to annatto. Lugaw is perfect for cold and rainy days, and is best served hot with freshly cracked black pepper and a squeeze of lime juice. Make a pot of lugaw for breakfast, lunch, or dinner, and top it off with Crunchy Garlic Chips (page 49) for added texture.

SERVES 4 TO 6

1 cup (195 g) white rice such as Calrose or Jasmine

1 medium onion, peeled

3 garlic cloves, peeled

1-inch (25 mm) piece fresh ginger, peeled (see Note)

2 tablespoons neutral oil such as vegetable, grapeseed, or avocado

7½ cups (1,800 ml) water

1 tablespoon annatto powder

Kosher salt and black pepper

1 scallion, trimmed and chopped, for serving

1 tablespoon Crunchy Garlic Chips (page 49), for serving

1 lime, cut into wedges, for serving

Rinse the rice two or three times in a fine-mesh strainer under cold water until the water runs clear. Set aside to drain. Finely chop the onion, mince the garlic, and thinly slice the ginger.

Heat the oil in a large pot over medium heat. Add the onions, garlic, and ginger and cook for 2 to 3 minutes, until soft.

Add the rice, water, annatto powder, and a generous pinch of salt and stir everything together until combined. Cover with a lid and simmer for 40 minutes, until the mixture thickens, stirring about every 15 minutes to prevent the rice from sticking to the bottom of the pot. Reduce the heat to low and simmer for another 10 to 20 minutes, until thick and creamy. Taste and adjust the salt as desired.

Serve with pepper, scallion, and garlic chips on top, with lime wedges for squeezing.

NOTE: *Peel the ginger using a teaspoon to scrape off the skin.*

Garlic Fried Rice

SINANGAG

In most Filipino households, you'll usually find sinangag served for breakfast with various types of protein and a fried egg. The combination has become such a staple combination that Filipinos invented a new word for it: silog. "Si" comes from "sinangag" (garlic fried rice) and "log" comes from "itlog," which means egg. Today, you'll find silog served at almost every corner restaurant in the Philippines; to make your own, see Freestyle It, below.

SERVES 2 TO 4

4 cups (600 g) cooked white rice (preferably day-old; see Note)

7 garlic cloves, peeled

3 tablespoons neutral oil such as vegetable, grapeseed, or avocado

Kosher salt

2 tablespoons toasted sesame oil

1 tablespoon Crunchy Garlic Chips (page 49)

Place the cooked rice in a large mixing bowl and sprinkle with about 2 tablespoons water. Using your hands, break the rice apart into small clusters. Set aside. (Skip this step if using freshly cooked rice.)

Mince the garlic.

Heat a large wok or heavy-bottomed skillet over medium-high heat. To check if the skillet is hot enough, add a drop of water; if you see it dancing around, let it evaporate and add the neutral oil. Add the garlic and a pinch of salt, and stir with a wooden spatula every few seconds. Once the garlic is lightly brown on the edges, reduce the heat to medium. Transfer half of the cooked garlic to a small bowl or ramekin and set aside.

Pour the sesame oil into the pan. Add the rice and quickly stir everything together. Season with a large pinch of salt and cook for 7 to 8 minutes, stirring every once in a while to make sure each grain is seasoned, until lightly toasted.

(continued)

Add the reserved cooked garlic and stir until the garlic is evenly distributed. Cook for an additional 2 to 3 minutes, until the garlic is evenly dispersed. Taste and adjust the seasoning as desired. Remove the pan from the heat and serve immediately, topped with the garlic chips.

NOTE: *For the best sinangag, use day-old rice instead of freshly cooked. Leftover rice has less moisture, which allows the grains to separate in the pan and fry evenly.*

Freestyle It

- You can make this into a plant-based version of silog by topping it with an omelet using Just Egg or your vegan egg of choice.
- Kick it up a notch by adding sautéed onions and mushrooms and serve it with a side salad.

Banana Ketchup Fried Rice

Banana ketchup, a sweeter, tangier version of the common condiment, is a staple in most Filipino pantries. This recipe calls for it to flavor the fried rice from the start instead of adding it as a condiment upon serving. Soy sauce and banana ketchup are both packed with umami, but the natural sugar and acidity from the ketchup helps curb soy sauce's sharp saltiness. The combination of sweet, tart, and savory flavors makes this dish similar in taste to pineapple fried rice.

SERVES 2 OR 3

1 small onion, peeled

3 garlic cloves, peeled

3 scallions, root ends trimmed off

2 cups (about 400 g) cooked rice (preferably day-old)

2 tablespoons neutral oil such as vegetable, grapeseed, or avocado

¼ cup (60 ml) banana ketchup

3 tablespoons soy sauce

Kosher salt

Chop the onion and mince the garlic; set both aside. Slice the scallions into thin rounds, and set the scallion whites and greens aside separately in ramekins or small bowls.

Place the cooked rice in a large mixing bowl and sprinkle in about 2 tablespoons water. Using your hands, break the rice apart into small clusters; set aside. (Skip this step if using freshly cooked rice.)

Heat the oil in a wok or heavy-bottomed skillet over medium-high heat for about 1 minute. Add the onions and cook for 2 to 3 minutes, until translucent. Add the white parts of the scallions and the garlic and cook for another 2 to 3 minutes, until soft. Add the cooked rice and stir until combined. Pour in the banana ketchup and soy sauce and add about a teaspoon of salt. Mix thoroughly until each rice grain is seasoned. Taste and adjust the seasoning as desired. Serve immediately, garnished with the scallion greens.

Filipino-Style Tofu Sausage

LONGGANISANG TOKWA

Longganisa is a sweet and garlicky Filipino sausage, often served as a side dish to rice for breakfast. This tofu-based version gets its fatty richness and umami from a combination of sesame oil and soy sauce. You'll make these sausages without a casing; instead, all-purpose flour and water help bind the tofu into shape.

MAKES 10 TO 12 SAUSAGES

1 block (14 ounces/400 g) extra firm tofu

1 bulb garlic, cloves separated and peeled

¼ cup (55 g) packed brown sugar

3 tablespoons toasted sesame oil

2 tablespoons soy sauce

2 tablespoons chili powder

2 tablespoons cane vinegar

¾ teaspoon kosher salt

1 teaspoon black pepper

¼ cup (30 g) all-purpose flour

¼ cup (60 ml) water

2 tablespoons neutral oil such as vegetable, canola, or avocado

Preheat the oven to 375°F (190°C). Line two rimmed baking sheets with aluminum foil.

Wrap the tofu in a clean kitchen towel or paper towel and place it on a rimmed plate or shallow bowl. Top with a heavy item like a cutting board and a large can of beans or tomatoes; let sit for at least 30 minutes to press out excess water. Unwrap and pat dry.

Crumble the tofu into a large mixing bowl in pea-sized pieces. Grate the garlic cloves into the same mixing bowl, using a Microplane or grater. Add the brown sugar, sesame oil, soy sauce, chili powder, vinegar, salt, and pepper. Mix together using your hands, making sure the tofu is evenly seasoned.

(continued)

Place the seasoned tofu on one of the lined baking sheets, spreading it out to ensure even cooking. Roast for 25 minutes, or until the tofu is crispy. Remove from the oven and let cool for 10 minutes.

Transfer the cooked tofu to a mixing bowl. Add the flour and water and stir together using a spatula until well combined. (The mixture should be thick and sticky.) Wet your hands with a bit of water to prevent the mixture from sticking to your hands. Scoop out 3 tablespoons of the tofu mixture and roll it into a ball between your palms. Carefully roll it into a 3-inch-long (8 cm) log. Place the sausages on the other prepared baking sheet. Repeat until you've used up the tofu mixture; you should have 10 to 12 sausages.

Add the neutral oil to a nonstick, cast-iron, or stainless-steel skillet and place it over medium-low heat. Drop in a small piece of the tofu mixture to check if the oil is hot enough. Once the oil bubbles around it, you should be good to fry. Working in batches, add as many sausages as you can fit into the pan, making sure they're not sticking to each other. Fry the sausages on each side for 3 to 4 minutes, until golden brown all over. Transfer to a wire rack or paper towel–lined plate to drain the excess oil. Serve immediately.

Store cooked leftovers in the freezer for up to 1 month, well wrapped, and thaw just before reheating.

Meal-ify It

› Serve with **Stovetop Coconut and Lemongrass Rice** (page 104) or steamed white rice (see page 103) and banana ketchup. Or pair with **Garlic Fried Rice** (page 21) and a quick **Green Mango Salad** (page 35) for a well-rounded meal.

Classic Avocado Smoothie

This sweet and creamy smoothie is a spin on abukado lamaw, a dessert that consists of mashed avocado, condensed milk, and ice. The avocado's high fat content imparts an inherently thick and silky texture to the smoothie; you may find it more akin to a milkshake.

SERVES 2

1 large avocado

1 cup (240 ml) plant-based milk such as oat or almond, chilled

3 ice cubes

2 tablespoons sweetened condensed plant-based milk or maple syrup, plus more if needed

Slice the avocado in half by piercing the fruit with a paring knife through the stem end, until the knife touches the pit. Keeping the knife against the pit, carefully rotate the avocado until it's sliced through. Twist the two halves apart. Place your index and middle finger around the pit, then push it out from behind using your thumb. Scoop out the flesh with a spoon and transfer it to a blender. Add the milk, ice cubes, and condensed milk and blend until smooth. Taste, adjust the sweetness, and blend again if needed. Pour into two glasses and serve immediately, while cold.

Silken Tofu with Sago Pearls and Syrup

TAHO

This pudding-like treat gets its soft, custardy texture not from dairy but from silken tofu. With chewy sago pearls and sweet syrup, this is an indulgent, sweet breakfast you can make at home. You can add a pandan leaf (sourced from any Asian supermarket) to the syrup for an extra nutty flavor. Make sure to yell "Taho! Taho!" when it's ready, just like the taho vendors shout in the Philippines.

SERVES 4 TO 6

1 cup (150 g) dried sago or mini tapioca pearls

1 package (14 ounces/400 g) soft silken tofu

1 packed cup (220 g) dark brown sugar

1 cup (240 ml) water

1 teaspoon pure vanilla extract

1 pandan leaf (optional)

Kosher salt

Bring a pot of water to a boil over medium-high heat. Add the sago pearls and stir. Cook for 15 minutes, or until the pearls are completely translucent. Drain the pearls in a fine-mesh strainer, rinse them in cold water, and set aside.

Remove the silken tofu from the package and drain off the liquid. Set up a bamboo steamer or metal steamer basket in a deep, wide pot with about ½ cup (120 ml) water in the bottom. Transfer the drained tofu to a heat-resistant plate, place the plate in the steamer, and cover it with a lid. Bring the water to a boil and steam for 6 to 7 minutes, until warm. Cut the tofu into thin slivers.

(continued)

Combine the brown sugar, water, vanilla, pandan leaf (if using), and a pinch of salt in a separate pot. Bring the mixture to a gentle simmer over low to medium heat and cook for 3 to 5 minutes, until the sugar has completely dissolved. Remove from heat.

Use heatproof glasses or clear parfait cups to assemble the taho. Place the tofu slivers at the bottom, using a slotted spoon. Next add a scoop of sago pearls and a tablespoon of syrup. Continue to layer in this order until you've reached the desired amount of taho. Gently stir the taho once to bring everything together, making sure not to destroy the textural integrity of the silken tofu. Enjoy while hot.

Store leftovers in the refrigerator for up to 2 days. Reheat in the microwave for 1 to 2 minutes or eat cold.

Mango-Coconut Smoothie

Frozen mango chunks are the key to achieving the light and luscious texture of this tropical smoothie. Incorporating coconut three different ways makes the drink creamy and nutty.

SERVES 2

- 2 tablespoons unsweetened coconut flakes
- 2 cups (280 g) frozen mango chunks
- 1 cup (240 ml) coconut milk, chilled
- 2 tablespoons maple syrup, plus more if needed
- 1 teaspoon pure vanilla extract
- 1 tablespoon whipped coconut cream

Spread out the coconut flakes evenly in a small skillet and place over medium-low heat. Toast for 2 to 3 minutes, until lightly golden, stirring occasionally to prevent them from burning. Remove from heat and set aside to cool.

Combine the mango chunks, coconut milk, maple syrup, and vanilla in a blender. Blend on high speed until smooth. Taste, adjust the sweetness, and blend again if needed. Pour the smoothie into two tall glasses. Serve with a dollop of whipped coconut cream and a sprinkle of golden coconut flakes on top.

Freestyle It

› Substitute frozen mango chunks with either 2 ripe yellow mangoes, such as Carabao or Ataúlfo, or frozen sliced peaches. For extra creaminess, you can also replace the maple syrup with sweetened condensed plant-based milk.

Salads, Starters & Staples

Every home cook can benefit from having some Filipino salads, condiments, and toppings in their arsenal. When you have a stocked pantry and fridge, cooking can be as simple as tossing a few components together and calling it a meal.

Meal-ify It

- For a simple tropical dinner, serve with lumpia (page 115, 119, 136, or 138) and **Stovetop Coconut and Lemongrass Rice** (page 104).

Green Mango Salad

ENSALADANG MANGGA

This salad comes together in no more than 15 minutes and has the perfect combination of sweet, salty, and sour. If serving it at a potluck or dinner party, you can make the salad ahead. It keeps well for several days, but note that the mangoes will soften as time passes.

SERVES 4 TO 6

2 green (unripe) mangoes

2 bell peppers, any color

1 medium red onion, peeled

2 tablespoons soy sauce

2 tablespoons freshly squeezed lime juice

Kosher salt and black pepper

Cut off the mango cheeks by standing each mango on end and slicing straight down along the seed. Lay each cheek skin side down on a cutting board and carefully scoop the fruit out using a large spoon, making sure to keep the whole cheek intact. Place the flat side down on the cutting board and slice the mango into ¼-inch (6 mm) pieces. Transfer to a mixing bowl.

Slice the tops off the bell peppers, then slice the peppers in half lengthwise. Remove the white membranes and seeds using a paring knife. Slice the peppers into thin vertical pieces and add them to the bowl with the mango.

Trim the root end off the onion. Stand the onion up on the flat end and cut it in half vertically. Lay the halves cut side down on the cutting board and thinly slice them. Add the onions to the bowl with the mango and bell pepper. Add the soy sauce, lime juice, and salt and pepper to taste. Toss to fully combine. Serve the salad fresh.

Transfer any leftovers to a tightly sealed container and store it in the refrigerator for up to 3 days.

Eggplant Salad

ENSALADANG TALONG

The combination of jammy soft eggplant, ripe tomatoes, and gently pickled red onions perfectly complement each other in this warm salad. Roasting eggplant with the skin on imparts a smokiness that sets it apart from any old ensaladang talong, so be sure not to skip that step. Use it as an accompaniment to any grilled or fried dish like Crispy Pan-Fried Tofu (page 46).

SERVES 2 TO 4

2 globe eggplants (about 15 ounces/450 g each)

1 tablespoon neutral oil such as vegetable, grapeseed, or avocado

Kosher salt and black pepper

1 Thai red chile

1 Roma tomato (about 2 ounces/60 g)

1 medium red onion, peeled

2 scallions, root ends trimmed off

2 teaspoons cane vinegar

Preheat the oven to 400°F (205°C). Line a rimmed baking sheet with aluminum foil.

Wash and dry the eggplants. Place the eggplants on the baking sheet. Using a fork, poke holes through each eggplant; this will allow steam to escape. Coat the eggplants with the oil. Season all sides with a pinch of salt and pepper. Roast the eggplants for 30 to 35 minutes, flipping halfway through. The eggplant is cooked when the flesh has fully collapsed and is tender enough to be easily mashed. Set aside to cool.

Cut the stem off the chile. Slice the chile in half lengthwise; remove the seeds if you want less heat. Finely chop the chile and add to a large mixing bowl. Chop the tomato, onion, and scallions into ½- to 1-inch-thick (1 to 2 cm) pieces and transfer them to the same mixing bowl. Toss everything together with a spoon.

When the eggplant has cooled for 5 to 10 minutes, peel off the skin. Transfer the eggplants to a large dinner plate and mash them with a fork while separating the threads. Add the mashed eggplant to the rest of the vegetables and season with the vinegar and salt and pepper to taste. Give everything a good mix, then taste and adjust the seasoning as needed. Serve immediately.

Freestyle It

- Keep the seeds in the chile peppers if you think you can handle more spice. Use rice vinegar if you don't have cane vinegar. If you have a gas stove, you can reduce the cooking time by charring the eggplant directly over a medium flame. Just hold off on adding oil and seasoning until *after* you've charred the eggplant, and make sure to flip the eggplant every couple of minutes to cook it evenly—you're looking for a jammy consistency on the inside and an almost burnt color on the outside.

Pomelo Salad

ENSALADANG POMELO

This refreshing 10-minute salad is inspired by yum som-o, a fragrant and citrusy Thai salad. Pomelo, the sweeter and mildly bitter sister of grapefruit, tastes extra refreshing alongside the array of herbs and greens. Its juices double as this salad's dressing, balancing the sweet and nutty notes from the brown sugar, soy sauce, and sesame oil. Pair this salad with any rich or fried dish and think of it as a palate cleanser.

SERVES 4

1 pomelo

1 red Thai chile

1 tablespoon soy sauce

1 tablespoon brown sugar

1 teaspoon toasted sesame oil

Juice of ½ lime

Kosher salt

¼ cup (34 g) raw, unsalted peanuts

¼ cup (4 g) loosely packed mint leaves

¼ cup (4 g) loosely packed cilantro leaves

¼ cup (4 g) loosely packed pea shoots

1 teaspoon Crunchy Garlic Chips (page 49)

Place the pomelo on a cutting board and slice off the top and bottom to expose the flesh. Position the fruit with one flat side down. Slice off the peel, making sure the knife hugs the fruit and follows its curved shape. Continue to remove the peel and pith by rotating the fruit. Carefully slice the fruit between the membranes to remove each segment. Transfer the pomelo segments to a mixing bowl.

Cut the stem off the chile. Slice the chile in half lengthwise; remove the seeds if you want less heat. Finely chop the chile and add to a small bowl. Add the soy sauce, brown sugar, sesame oil, lime juice, and a heavy pinch of salt. Stir everything together to combine, then set aside.

(continued)

Finely chop the peanuts on the cutting board and transfer them to a small skillet. Toast the peanuts over medium-high heat for 2 to 3 minutes, until lightly golden brown. Stir the peanuts occasionally to prevent them from burning. Remove from heat and transfer them to a separate small bowl.

Roughly tear the mint and cilantro leaves by hand directly into the bowl with the pomelo. Add the pea shoots, dressing, and half of the peanuts. Toss everything together by hand and season with salt to taste. To serve, transfer the salad to a serving bowl and sprinkle on the garlic chips and the remainder of the peanuts.

Quick Pan-Fried Eggplant in Soy Sauce

PRITONG TALONG

This five-ingredient recipe uses just a handful of pantry staples to create the ultimate low-effort/high-reward type of dish. The combination of soy sauce and the subtle sweetness of the fried eggplant tastes harmonious enough to stand alone without further seasonings or ingredients. Serve it with steamed rice and you have yourself a perfect lazy meal.

SERVES 2 TO 4

2 Chinese eggplants (about 20 ounces/600 g total)

3 tablespoons neutral oil such as vegetable, grapeseed, or avocado

¼ cup (60 ml) soy sauce

1 teaspoon freshly squeezed lime juice

Steamed white rice (see page 103), for serving

Slice the eggplants lengthwise into quarters and then cut in half crosswise.

Heat the oil in a heavy-bottomed skillet over medium-high heat. Once the oil is shimmering hot, carefully place the eggplants in the pan and fry each side for 4 to 5 minutes, until tender and cooked through. Lightly brush each side with soy sauce as you flip. Remove the cooked eggplants from the heat and transfer to a serving plate.

Add the lime juice to the remaining soy sauce to use as the dipping sauce. Serve the fried eggplants while hot with white rice.

Meal-ify It

- You can toss the cooked eggplant in a grain bowl along with **Crispy Pan-Fried Tofu** (page 46), shelled edamame, shredded carrots, sesame seeds, and a drizzle of hot sauce for an extra kick.

Tangy Pickled Papaya

ATCHARA

Atchara (or atsara) are refrigerator pickles made with green (unripe) papaya. They're sweet and puckery, and get a slight kick from black peppercorns. Often served with fried or grilled foods, they provide mouth-watering tang to balance the savory notes of stir-fries and grilled dishes. You can make them on the fly or days ahead of time—just make sure they soak in the brine for at least an hour.

MAKES 5 TO 6 CUPS (1.2 TO 1.4 L)

1 green (unripe) papaya (about 24 ounces/680 g), peeled and seeded

3 tablespoons plus ½ teaspoon kosher salt

1⅓ cups (315 ml) cane vinegar

⅔ cup (160 g) packed brown sugar

1 large carrot, peeled

1 red bell pepper

6 garlic cloves, peeled

1-inch (2.5 cm) piece fresh ginger, peeled

1 tablespoon black peppercorns

Dried bay leaves

Shred the papaya by scraping it against the large holes of a box grater, carefully moving it from top to bottom to create long, thin strips. Transfer the papaya shreds to a large mixing bowl and add 3 tablespoons of the salt. Mix thoroughly using your hands, cover, and set aside for 40 minutes to allow the papaya to expel excess liquid.

Simmer the vinegar in a small saucepan over medium-high heat for 3 minutes or until it boils. Reduce the heat to medium-low and add the brown sugar and the remaining ½ teaspoon salt. Stir together and remove from heat as soon as the sugar dissolves. Set aside.

Shred the carrot on the box grater's large holes and set aside in a separate large mixing bowl. Slice the top off the bell pepper, then slice the pepper in half lengthwise. Remove the white membranes and seeds using a paring knife. Slice the pepper into thin vertical pieces and add them to the bowl

(continued)

with the carrot. Thinly slice the garlic cloves and ginger and add to the carrot and bell pepper.

Transfer the papaya to a fine-mesh strainer or mesh spider and rinse under cold water. Drain, then squeeze out as much water as you can. Add the papaya to the carrots, bell pepper, garlic, and ginger. Add black peppercorns and brine and mix together thoroughly for 5 minutes.

Pack the vegetables into clean jars with lids and tuck a couple of bay leaves into each jar. Pour in enough of the brine to cover by ½ inch (1 cm). Let the vegetables completely cool at room temperature for about 15 minutes, then cover the jars with their lids. Transfer to the refrigerator where the pickles will keep for up to 2 months.

Multipurpose Tofu Crumbles

These tofu crumbles resemble crushed chicharron (pork cracklings) and add a crunchy finish to any dish—think soups, stir-fries, salads, and noodles. Extracting as much water from the tofu as possible and breaking it into tiny pieces will help ensure your crumbles come out perfectly brown and crispy.

SERVES 4 TO 6

1 block (14 ounces/400 g) extra firm tofu

¼ cup (60 ml) neutral oil such as vegetable, grapeseed, or avocado

½ teaspoon kosher salt, or more if needed

Wrap the tofu in a clean kitchen towel and place it on a rimmed plate or shallow bowl. Top with a heavy item like a cutting board; let sit for at least 30 minutes to press out excess water. Unwrap and break into fine little crumbles.

Line a rimmed baking sheet with several layers of paper towels.

Heat the oil in a large heavy-bottomed skillet over medium-high. Gently place the crumbled tofu in the pan, making sure to spread it evenly. Fry for 8 to 10 minutes, until the bottom starts to crisp up. Toss to let the other side crisp up and cook for another 10 minutes. Remove from heat.

Transfer the crumbles to the prepared baking sheet to drain the excess oil. Season with salt to taste and toss together by hand to season evenly.

Store any leftover crumbles in a tightly covered jar for up to 3 days.

Freestyle It

› To flavor the tofu crumbles, toss them with soy sauce, salt, and pepper before frying; add them to any savory dish for an extra bite. You could also add other seasonings such as garlic powder and chili powder right after frying; serve the tofu crumbles in tacos, wraps, and grain bowls.

Crispy Pan-Fried Tofu

The key to getting tofu crispy without coating it with cornstarch is patience—but it really doesn't take *too* long. Use pan-fried tofu in Mung Bean Stew (page 63), Vegetable Noodle Soup (page 69), or in a simple vegetable stir-fry that could do with some extra protein.

SERVES 2 OR 3

1 block (14 ounces/400 g) extra firm tofu

¼ cup (60 ml) toasted sesame oil

2 tablespoons soy sauce or tamari

Freshly cracked black pepper

Wrap the tofu in a clean kitchen towel or paper towel and place it on a rimmed plate or shallow bowl. Top with a heavy item like a cutting board and a large can of beans or tomatoes; let sit for at least 30 minutes to press out excess water. Unwrap and pat dry.

Break the tofu apart into 1-inch (2.5 cm) chunks using your hands. Doing this will give the tofu crispier edges, which is the whole point of this recipe!

Heat the oil in a large heavy-bottomed skillet over medium-high heat. Once the oil is shimmering hot, gently place the tofu pieces in the pan one by one, working in batches if necessary to avoid overcrowding the pan. Fry each side for 4 to 5 minutes, until golden brown and crispy all over.

Reduce the heat to medium-low and pour the soy sauce directly in the hot pan with the tofu. Toss together until each tofu piece is seasoned. Fry for another 3 to 4 minutes, stirring after about 2 minutes to even out the color and texture of the tofu. If the oil splatters, cover the pan. Remove from heat, season with pepper to taste, and serve while hot.

Meal-ify It

- This tofu can be added to just about any stir-fried dish or stew served with either rice or noodles. Simplify it even more by serving the tofu alongside steamed vegetables such as broccoli or bok choy for an easy weeknight meal.

Daily Dipping Sauce

SAWSAWAN

Grilled or fried Filipino food is best served with a side of sawsawan, a spicy, savory, and sour sauce. You'll find sawsawan at every street food stall in the Philippines, to be eaten with the crispy Vegetable Spring Rolls we call lumpia (page 115) or the Crunchy Vegetable Fritters known as okoy (page 125). You can customize this recipe depending on how spicy or sour you want it to be, but use these proportions as a starting point.

MAKES ABOUT 1½ CUPS (360 ML); SERVES 4 TO 6

1 small red onion, peeled

1 red Thai chile

1 garlic clove, peeled

1 cup (240 ml) cane vinegar or rice vinegar

1 tablespoon soy sauce

Finely chop the red onion and place in a small bowl. Cut the stem off the chile. Slice the chile in half lengthwise; remove the seeds if you want less heat. Finely chop the chile and add to bowl with the onion. Slice the garlic into paper-thin pieces and add to the bowl. Pour in the vinegar and soy sauce. Stir everything together to combine. Use the sauce immediately.

Store leftovers in an airtight container for up to a month in the refrigerator.

Crunchy Garlic Chips

Garlic is at the core of most, if not all, savory Filipino dishes. These garlic chips provide an addicting kick to any soup, stew, or stir-fried dish. Sprinkle this on top of anything that needs an extra bit of crunch.

MAKES ABOUT ½ CUP (30 G)

1 bulb garlic, papery outer skin removed, separated into cloves

⅓ cup (80 ml) neutral oil such as vegetable, grapeseed, or avocado

Kosher salt

Place the garlic cloves in a jar or a small container and cover tightly with a lid. Shake the jar vigorously for 30 to 40 seconds. This will peel the garlic without your having to do each clove by hand. Once the skin is off the cloves, cut off the little hard nub, if necessary, and slice the garlic lengthwise into paper-thin chips.

Heat the oil in a small saucepan over medium heat. Once the oil is hot, add the garlic and fry for 5 to 6 minutes, until golden brown. Make sure to stir the garlic occasionally to prevent it from burning. Remove the fried garlic using a slotted spoon, a mesh spider, or a fine-mesh strainer and transfer to a small mixing bowl lined with paper towels. Shake the bowl gently to remove excess oil.

Season the garlic chips with salt to taste and gently toss them by hand to make sure each one is seasoned.

Use immediately or store the garlic chips in an airtight container at room temperature for up to 5 days.

NOTE: *Reserve the remaining garlic oil in a small jar to use in other savory dishes. This should keep for 2 to 3 weeks at room temperature.*

Golden Coconut Curd

TAGALOG LATIK

Latik is a sweet, crunchy, and golden brown topping made with coconut cream and brown sugar. Traditionally, it's used as a garnish for sweet Filipino delicacies, but you can also use it as a topping for desserts like ice cream or cake, or even yogurt. This recipe only uses two ingredients—plus you get coconut oil as a result of the cooking process. It's a gift that keeps on giving!

MAKES 1 CUP (90 G)

2 cans (about 14 ounces/400 g each) coconut cream

2½ tablespoons brown sugar

Pour the coconut cream into a large saucepan. Place over medium heat and cook for 20 minutes or until it starts to boil. Reduce the heat to low and simmer the cream for another 10 to 15 minutes, stirring occasionally. You'll notice the cream start to curdle. Once the coconut curds separate from the oil, leave the saucepan on the heat for another 5 to 6 minutes, until the curds turn golden brown. Remove from heat as soon as the curds turn brown.

At this point, the curds should sink to the bottom of the pan and the remaining coconut oil should be clear. Separate them by pouring into a fine-mesh strainer set over a small bowl. Store the coconut oil in an airtight jar at room temperature to use for other recipes. Transfer the coconut curds to a medium-large mixing bowl.

While the coconut curds are still warm, add the brown sugar and stir together until the curds and sugar are fully combined.

Use immediately or store in an airtight container in the refrigerator for up to 2 weeks.

Stews & Soups

Stews, soups, and stir-fries make up the fundamental formats of Filipino dishes. No matter what you crave, from vegetable-packed coconut-spiked soups to quick and easy stir-fries, you can make nourishing, soul-satisfying dishes with simple ingredients you likely already have on hand.

Low-and-Slow Vegetable Stew

AFRITADANG GULAY

Nothing says cozy soup season more than a warm bowl of fork-tender vegetables in a hearty broth. This plant-based version of a classic beef stew is tinged with sugar, spice, and everything nice (that is, garlic and soy sauce). Take your time when cooking this stew to let the potatoes release their starch and contribute a velvety mouthfeel in every slurp of broth. Serve the stew with steamed white rice for a classic comfort meal.

SERVES 4 TO 6

- 1 large carrot (about 5 ounces/150 g), peeled
- 2 yellow potatoes (about 7 ounces/200 g each)
- 1 red bell pepper
- 1 small onion, peeled
- 4 garlic cloves, peeled
- 1 tablespoon neutral oil such as vegetable, canola, or avocado
- 1 teaspoon kosher salt
- 1 can (28 ounces/794 g) tomato sauce or crushed tomatoes
- 1 dried bay leaf
- 1½ tablespoons brown sugar
- 1 tablespoon soy sauce
- ½ teaspoon black pepper
- Stovetop Coconut and Lemongrass Rice (page 104) or steamed white rice (see page 103), for serving

Remove and discard the root and stem ends of the carrot, then slice the carrot into ½-inch-thick (1 cm) rounds. Slice the bigger pieces into half-moons to ensure each piece cooks evenly. Peel the potatoes, discarding the skins. Cut the potatoes into cubes, then place them in a bowl and cover with water. Slice the top off the bell pepper, then slice the pepper in half lengthwise. Remove the white membranes and seeds using a paring knife. Slice the pepper into thin vertical strips. Chop the onion and mince the garlic cloves.

(continued)

Pour the oil into a heavy-bottomed pot and warm over medium-high heat. When the oil is shimmering hot, add the onions and cook until translucent, 2 to 3 minutes. Add the garlic and cook for another 2 minutes or until soft. Add the carrots, season with some of the salt, and stir everything together until combined. Cook the carrots for about 10 minutes, until slightly tender on the outside, stirring occasionally to ensure they don't stick to the bottom of the pot.

Drain the potatoes and add them to the pot. Season with salt again and stir to combine. Cook for another 6 minutes, until everything is combined and well seasoned, stirring occasionally to ensure nothing sticks to the bottom of the pot.

Add the tomatoes and bay leaf and stir until combined. Reduce the heat to medium, then cover the pot with a lid and simmer for 20 minutes or until the vegetables are fork-tender.

Add the brown sugar, soy sauce, and pepper, and stir until combined. Add the bell peppers and stir again. Taste the sauce and adjust the seasoning if needed. Cook for another 12 to 15 minutes with the lid on, until all the vegetables are tender. Remove from heat and serve immediately with a bowl of steamed rice.

Squash and Green Bean–Coconut Stew

GINATAANG KALABASA AT SITAW

The simple combination of tender squash and crunchy green beans in a coconut-based sauce creates a perfect bite, thanks to its balance of contrasting flavors and textures. Top it with Crispy Pan-Fried Tofu (page 46) for extra heft (and crunch) and serve the stew with steamed white rice for a classic Filipino-style meal.

SERVES 4 TO 6

1 small kabocha or medium acorn squash (about 2 pounds/ 900 grams), well scrubbed

11 ounces (330 g) green beans

5 garlic cloves, peeled

1 large onion, peeled

1 tablespoon neutral oil such as vegetable, canola, or avocado

1½ teaspoons kosher salt

1 can (400 ml) coconut milk

2 tablespoons soy sauce

½ teaspoon black pepper

Crispy Pan-Fried Tofu (page 46)

Stovetop Coconut and Lemongrass Rice (page 104) or steamed white rice (see page 103), for serving

Place the squash on a cutting board on its bottom (blossom end). Using a sharp chef's knife, pierce the squash across the top at the center, then carefully slice it in half with a rocking motion. Once you're halfway through, use your other hand to help push the knife down until the squash splits in half. Scoop out the seeds and fibers; discard them, or store in an airtight container to roast later. Place the flat, cut side down on the cutting board and cut the kabocha into 1-inch-thick (2.5 cm) wedges. If the stem or hard blossom end are still attached to the ends of wedges, cut them off. Chop the wedges into cubes. Set aside in a large mixing bowl.

(continued)

Lay the green beans on the cutting board and align the tips. Cut off and discard the stems and tips; set the green beans aside in a separate bowl. Mince the garlic cloves and chop the onion.

Heat the oil in a large saucepan over medium heat. Add the onions, stir, and cook for 2 to 3 minutes, until translucent. Add the garlic; stir and cook for 1 minute or until just soft.

Add the squash and a pinch of the salt and cook for 6 to 7 minutes, until the edges of the squash start to soften. Stir occasionally to ensure nothing sticks to the bottom of the saucepan. If anything sticks, add 1 tablespoon water and gently scrape up the bottom of the pan.

Add the coconut milk and soy sauce, stir, and reduce the heat to medium-low. Cover the saucepan with a lid and simmer for 10 to 12 minutes, until the squash is fork-tender.

Add the green beans and pepper and stir to combine. Taste the sauce and adjust the seasoning with more salt or soy sauce. Re-cover the pot and simmer for another 5 to 7 minutes, until the beans are fork-tender.

Add the tofu and gently stir until the tofu is covered with sauce. Remove from heat and serve immediately with steamed rice.

Store any leftovers for up to 2 days in the refrigerator in an airtight container, or freeze them for up to a month.

Freestyle It

- Instead of using kabocha squash, you can use 2 sweet potatoes, peeled and chopped into cubes. Add any hearty leafy vegetables you like, such as kale and spinach, for extra greens. Serve with steamed rice and a teaspoon of your favorite chili crisp for an extra kick.

Creamy Jackfruit-Coconut Stew

GINATAANG LANGKA

Using canned jackfruit makes this stew an easy and quick pantry dish to throw together. While vegan recipes often employ jackfruit to emulate pulled meat in sandwiches or tacos, this recipe will show you that jackfruit shines in its own right without being disguised as something it is not. Include other vegetables or proteins to add some more heft to this soup. If you can't find canned jackfruit, feel free to freestyle this recipe with chickpeas as instructed below.

SERVES 2 TO 4

1 can (20 ounces/565 g) green jackfruit, drained

5 garlic cloves, peeled

1 large onion, peeled

1-inch (2.5 cm) piece fresh ginger, peeled

1 tablespoon neutral oil such as vegetable, canola, or avocado

Kosher salt and black pepper

1 can (400 ml) coconut milk

1 teaspoon soy sauce

Stovetop Coconut and Lemongrass Rice (page 104) or steamed white rice (see page 103), for serving

Rinse the jackfruit under cold water; drain and set aside. Mince the garlic, chop the onion, and slice the ginger into thin rounds.

Heat the oil in a medium saucepan over medium heat. Add the onions and cook for 2 to 3 minutes, until translucent. Add the garlic and ginger, then season with a pinch of salt and stir together until combined. Cook for another 3 minutes; add the jackfruit and coconut milk. Season with the soy sauce, about a teaspoon of salt, and half a teaspoon of pepper, and stir until thoroughly combined. Cover the pot with a lid, reduce the heat to medium-low, and simmer for 10 minutes or until the jackfruit softens. Taste the sauce and adjust the seasoning as needed, then remove from heat and serve immediately with a bowl of steamed rice.

Freestyle It

- Use one 19-ounce (540 g) can chickpeas, drained, as an alternative to jackfruit. Toast the chickpeas with the alliums until lightly golden before adding the coconut milk. Simmer until the chickpeas have absorbed some of that nuttiness from the coconut milk. Before removing from the heat, add a large handful of spinach or your choice of soft greens and stir everything together. The spinach should wilt down in no time, so you can immediately serve the stew after combining everything together.

Mung Bean Stew

GINISANG MUNGGO

In addition to classic pantry legumes like chickpeas, lentils, and black beans, the humble mung bean, or munggo, is a slightly sweet and buttery legume that's just as packed in nutrients as its siblings. Here the mung beans are gently simmered until soft, which allows them to absorb layers of umami from the tomato, soy sauce, and ginger. Combined with spinach, alliums, and Crispy Pan-Fried Tofu (page 46), this nutrient-dense stew becomes a filling and nuanced meal alongside some steamed rice.

SERVES 4 TO 6

1 cup (195 g) dried mung beans

1 large onion, peeled

6 garlic cloves, peeled

1 Roma tomato (about 2 ounces/60 g)

1-inch (2.5 cm) piece fresh ginger, peeled

1½ teaspoons neutral oil such as vegetable, canola, or avocado

Kosher salt and black pepper

6 cups (1.4 L) water

2 tablespoons soy sauce

5 cups (100 g) loosely packed spinach leaves

Crispy Pan-Fried Tofu (page 46)

Stovetop Coconut and Lemongrass Rice (page 104) or steamed white rice (see page 103), for serving

Rinse the beans, transfer them to a bowl, and cover with water. Leave to soak for about 1 hour, then drain.

Chop the onion and mince the garlic cloves. Slice the tomato in half lengthwise and chop into ½- to 1-inch (1 to 2 cm) pieces; do not remove the seeds. Slice the ginger into thin rounds.

Heat the oil in a large pot over medium-high. Add the onions and cook for 2 to 3 minutes, until translucent. Add the garlic, tomatoes, and ginger and season with a generous pinch of salt. Cook for about 3 minutes, until the tomatoes are soft.

(continued)

Add the beans, season with a pinch of salt, and stir to combine. Add 4 cups (960 ml) of the water and reduce the heat to low. Cover with a lid and simmer for about 20 minutes, until the beans are fork-tender.

Gently crush a few of the beans using the bottom of a ladle; this will give the stew more body and richness without any other thickener or milk. Pour in the remaining water and the soy sauce, re-cover the pot, and simmer for another 15 minutes, until the beans are soft and slightly falling apart. Add salt and pepper to taste. Add the spinach and mix everything until combined. Remove the pan from the heat and leave the pot covered for another 5 minutes to let the spinach wilt. Add the tofu and top with more pepper. Serve immediately with steamed rice.

Freestyle It

- Use green lentils as an alternative to mung beans. Top with **Crispy Pan-Fried Tofu** (page 46) or simply slice a block of tofu into ½- to 1-inch (1 to 2 cm) pieces and add directly into the pot before the spinach. Add more water for a soupier base and adjust the seasoning with more salt and pepper to taste.

Hearty Peanut Stew

KARE KARE

The addition of peanut butter makes this stew velvety smooth. Traditional kare kare is slow-cooked and accompanied by an array of vegetables like bok choy, eggplant, and long beans. The stew's flavors come together with the sweetness of the vegetables combining with the umami of the garlic and soy sauce. Serve kare kare with steamed white rice or add cooked rice noodles for a belly-warming meal.

SERVES 4 TO 6

1 pound (450 g) baby bok choy

1 Chinese eggplant, or ½ globe eggplant (about 7.5 ounces/225 g)

1 bunch (5 ounces/150 g) long beans

1 large onion, peeled

3 garlic cloves, peeled

2 tablespoons peanut butter

1½ cups (360 ml) water

1 tablespoon neutral oil such as vegetable, canola, or avocado

3 tablespoons soy sauce

Kosher salt and black pepper

Stovetop Coconut and Lemongrass Rice (page 104) or steamed white rice (see page 103), for serving

Cut off and discard the base of each head of bok choy. Rinse the bok choy well to remove any dirt from between the leaves. Set aside to drain well.

Cut off the eggplant stem, then cut the eggplant on the bias into slices ½ to 1 inch thick (1 to 2 cm). Align the bottom ends of the long beans and trim them off. Working in batches, slice the long beans into 3-inch (8 cm) pieces. Chop the onion and mince the garlic cloves. Combine the peanut butter with 1 tablespoon of the water in a small bowl. Stir until smooth.

Heat the oil in a large saucepan over medium-high heat. When the oil begins to shimmer, add the onions and garlic. Cook for 2 to 3 minutes, until the onions are translucent; it's okay if the edges brown a little.

Add the long beans and cook for 2 to 3 minutes, until tender. Add the eggplant and season with soy sauce, about a teaspoon of salt, and half

(continued)

a teaspoon of pepper and mix to combine. Add the peanut butter mixture and the rest of the water and stir. Reduce the heat to medium-low, cover the pot, and simmer for 7 to 8 minutes, until the sauce has slightly reduced and thickened.

Taste the broth and add more salt and pepper as needed. Add the bok choy and stir until it's submerged in the liquid. Cover the pot again and simmer for another 5 to 6 minutes, until the vegetables are fork-tender. Remove from heat and serve immediately with steamed rice.

Freestyle It

› Make rice noodles instead of steamed rice to serve for a creamy, vegetable-packed dish to slurp on. For plating, simply add the cooked and drained noodles at the bottom of your bowl, then ladle a couple of servings of the kare kare on top.

Vegetable Noodle Soup

SOTANGHON

This comforting noodle soup is packed with vegetables, aromatics like fried onions and grated garlic, and a dash of sesame oil. Each vegetable is sliced to a size that ensures that every spoonful captures all the goodness in one bite. Traditional sotanghon is usually made with cellophane noodles, which you can use in this recipe if you prefer, but chewier, thicker sweet potato noodles add a subtle sweetness and toothsome bite.

SERVES 4 TO 6

3 garlic cloves, peeled

1 large onion, peeled

1 scallion, root end trimmed off

4 ounces (120 g) cremini mushrooms

4 ounces (110 g) green beans

5 napa cabbage leaves (preferably the large outer leaves)

1 large carrot, peeled

1 tablespoon neutral oil such as vegetable, grapeseed, or avocado

Kosher salt and black pepper

4 cups (960 ml) water

1 tablespoon soy sauce

1 package (8 ounces/250 g) sweet potato glass noodles

2 teaspoons toasted sesame oil

Crispy Pan-Fried Tofu (page 46)

Grate the garlic cloves into a small bowl using a Microplane or grater. Slice the onion in half and chop into ½-inch (1 cm) pieces; set aside. Finely chop the scallion and set aside separately.

Clean the mushrooms using a clean kitchen towel to brush off the dirt (see page 98). Slice them into ½-inch (1 cm) pieces and transfer them to a clean baking sheet. Working in batches, align a handful of green beans on a cutting board and trim off the tips and stems. Slice the green beans on the bias to the same thickness as the mushrooms and set aside in a separate pile on the same baking sheet. Chop the cabbage into ½- to 1-inch (1 to 2 cm) pieces and transfer to the baking sheet,

(continued)

making a third pile. Slice the carrot on the bias about ¼ inch (6 mm) thick. Working in batches, stack a few carrot slices and cut them into thin matchsticks; set aside separately.

Heat the neutral oil in a large pot over medium heat. Add the onions and cook for about 2 minutes, until translucent. Add the green beans and season with a pinch of salt. Cook for about 1 minute, until glossy. Add the carrots and cook them for another 1 minute, until glossy. Add the garlic and mix thoroughly to combine. Add the water, season with the soy sauce and a pinch of salt and pepper, and then bring to a boil.

Add the noodles to the pot of boiling soup, making sure they're completely submerged in the liquid. Reduce the heat to medium-low, cover the pot with a lid, and let the noodles cook for 8 to 10 minutes, until they're tender but not too soft.

Add the sesame oil, mushrooms, and cabbage, and stir. Taste the soup and adjust the seasoning as needed. Continue to simmer for another 3 to 4 minutes, until the cabbage and mushrooms are cooked through. Add the tofu and stir to combine. Serve the soup hot, ladling it into bowls and garnishing with scallions.

Freestyle It

› You can replace the sweet potato noodles with any type of rice vermicelli. Cook it for the time suggested on the package. If you're looking for an extra kick, drizzle sriracha to your heart's desire and add a sprinkle of **Crunchy Garlic Chips** (page 49) for extra texture and flavor.

Earthy Mushroom Noodle Soup

MUSHROOM BATCHOY

While mushrooms are the star of this batchoy, garlic takes the award for best supporting role. In addition to fresh garlic, this recipe calls for Crunchy Garlic Chips (page 49), adding an extra layer of aromatic nuttiness. The oyster mushrooms are coated in potato starch and fried until crispy, while the enoki mushrooms are cooked in the broth, creating a contrasting variety of textures. Make this soup for guests for a crowd-pleasing meal served with Sizzling Mushroom and Tofu Sisig (page 101) and Quick Pan-Fried Eggplant in Soy Sauce (page 41).

SERVES 4 TO 6

- 7 ounces (200 g) oyster mushrooms
- 5 ounces (150 g) enoki mushrooms
- ¼ cup (38 g) potato starch or (30 g) glutinous rice flour
- 6 garlic cloves, peeled
- 2 scallions, root ends trimmed off
- 1 red Thai chile
- Neutral oil such as vegetable, grapeseed, or avocado
- Kosher salt
- 4 cups (960 ml) water
- 2 tablespoons soy sauce
- 1 tablespoon toasted sesame oil
- ½ teaspoon MSG (optional)
- 9 ounces (230 g) thin wheat flour noodles
- 2 tablespoons Crunchy Garlic Chips (page 49) or store-bought fried garlic
- 2 tablespoons Multipurpose Tofu Crumbles (page 45)

Gently break the oyster mushrooms apart into large, flat pieces. Clean the oyster mushrooms and enoki mushrooms by brushing off any dirt using a kitchen towel, or quickly rinse them with cold water, then immediately dry (see page 98). Place the oyster mushrooms in a large mixing bowl. Add the potato starch and gently toss together with your hands until the mushrooms are well coated.

(continued)

Trim the bottom roots of the enoki mushrooms, if there are any, and gently shred the cluster of mushrooms into smaller pieces using your hands. Set aside in a small bowl. Thinly slice the garlic cloves crosswise. Slice the scallions into thin rounds. Cut the stem off the chile. Slice the chile in half lengthwise; remove the seeds if you want less heat. Finely chop the chile. Set everything aside.

Cover the bottom of a 10-inch (25 cm) skillet with a thin layer of neutral oil and heat over medium-high heat. Once the oil is shimmering hot, reduce the heat to medium and fry the oyster mushrooms for 5 to 6 minutes, until crispy on all sides. Make sure not to overcrowd the pan, because potato starch has the tendency to cause things to stick to each other; work in batches if necessary. Transfer the oyster mushrooms to a wire rack with a slotted spoon or mesh spider and let them cool. Once cool, roughly chop them into ½- to 1-inch (1 to 2 cm) pieces and set aside.

While the mushrooms are cooling, heat about 2 tablespoons neutral oil in a large pot over medium-high heat. Add the garlic and cook for 2 minutes or until tender. Add the enoki mushrooms and cook for 4 to 5 minutes, until the mushrooms are slightly browned. Season with a generous pinch of salt.

Add the water, soy sauce, sesame oil, and MSG, if using, to the pot. Bring to a boil, add the noodles, and stir together. Reduce the heat and simmer until the noodles are al dente, about 3 minutes. Taste the soup and adjust the seasoning as needed. Add half of the chopped oyster mushrooms and stir together. Remove from heat.

Serve in bowls, topped with the remaining chopped oyster mushrooms, some scallions, garlic chips, and tofu crumbles.

The History of Batchoy and Regional Cooking in the Philippines

In the 1930s, the La Paz Public Market in Iloilo City was a hub for manual laborers stopping by during their breaks. According to tales told by Ilonggo elders, the laborers always seemed tired, eating meals that didn't give them enough fuel to work. The market and eatery owners realized the need for a hearty, nourishing meal that wasn't just lugaw (congee or rice porridge), hence the birth of batchoy. Some claim that batchoy was inspired by Chinese noodle soups sold in Molo, the Chinatown of Iloilo.

At its core, batchoy is a pork noodle soup, but its complexity lies in the layers of flavor, which can be recreated in a plant-based rendition. The rich and hearty broth is a testament to the Chinese influence on Filipino cooking, as Chinese migrants brought the art of noodle making and savory broths to the country.

The melding of Chinese cooking techniques with local ingredients led to a distinctive Filipino version of the soup. Central to batchoy is the use of miki noodles, a type of egg noodle reminiscent of Chinese mien. The soup is then topped with different meats, such as pork shoulder and offal, creating a medley of textures and flavors while providing sustenance to the hardworking people stopping by the market.

As batchoy migrated from the streets of La Paz to kitchens across the Philippines, its cultural significance expanded. Today, it is not just a bowl of soup; it's a dish ingrained in Filipino history. This is particularly evident in how regional variations of batchoy have emerged, each reflective of the unique culinary landscapes and preferences within the archipelago.

In the Visayan region, batchoy uses guinamos, a local shrimp paste, adding a distinct coastal flavor to the broth. In Manila, one of the most densely populated cities in the world, flavors from various regions in the Philippines meet. The influence of migrants from across the country and tourists have led to variations including the addition of crushed chicharron (pork cracklings) for an extra layer of crunch and flavor. These regional adaptations showcase the dynamic nature of Filipino cuisine, where local ingredients and preferences shape the evolution of a dish.

Using this approach, traditional Filipino batchoy can be transformed into a plant-based delight, swapping out meat for fried earthy mushrooms to achieve a robust umami flavor, and embracing sesame oil to add depth and richness.

Filipino Wonton Soup

PANCIT MOLO

Hand-crafted dumplings swimming in a warm broth is a dish typically served in the Philippines on special occasions like Christmas and New Year's Eve, but who is to say you can't make these festive wontons year-round? If you're in a rush or need a quick snack, using store-bought wontons from your local Asian market does the trick. The broth is simple, but the toasted sesame oil adds an extra layer of umami and fattiness that really takes this dish to the next level.

MAKES ABOUT 30 WONTONS; SERVES 4 TO 6

WONTONS

9 ounces (260 g) extra firm tofu (about ⅔ of a 14-ounce/400 g block), cubed

4 ounces (120 g) cremini mushrooms

½ medium carrot, peeled

1 medium onion, peeled

1-inch (2.5 cm) piece fresh ginger, peeled

3 garlic cloves, peeled

5 scallions, root ends trimmed off

Kosher salt and black pepper

1 package (12 ounces/340 g) 3 × 3-inch (8 × 8 cm) wonton wrappers

SOUP

4 cups (960 ml) water

2 tablespoons toasted sesame oil

2 tablespoons soy sauce

1 tablespoon store-bought fried garlic or Crunchy Garlic Chips (page 49)

Chili crisp, for serving (optional)

Wrap the tofu in a clean kitchen towel or paper towel and place it on a rimmed plate or shallow bowl. Top with a heavy item like a cutting board and a large can of beans or tomatoes; let it sit for at least 30 minutes to press out excess water. Unwrap and pat dry. Break the tofu into fine little crumbles and transfer it to a large mixing bowl.

Finely chop the mushrooms, carrot, onion, ginger, and garlic and combine them with the tofu. Finely chop the scallions; set aside 2 tablespoons for garnish later and add the rest to the other vegetables. Season the vegetables with about a teaspoon of salt and half a teaspoon of pepper, and mix to combine.

Prepare about ½ cup of water in a ramekin to use for sealing the wontons. Place a wonton wrapper in the palm of your nondominant hand with a point facing you. Place a teaspoon of the vegetable filling in the center. Take the bottom corner of the wrapper, dip your finger in water, dab the edges, and fold it over to meet the top end, pressing the edges firmly to seal. Dab a bit of water on the right and left corners of the wrapper, and then take each corner and press them together to create another seal. Place the finished wonton on a baking sheet and repeat until you've finished all the filling. (If you have any wrappers left, wrap the package well in plastic or put it in a heavy resealable bag or airtight container, and put them back in the freezer for another time.)

Bring the water for the soup to a boil in a large pot over medium heat. Add the sesame oil, soy sauce, fried garlic, a heavy pinch of salt, and about half a teaspoon of pepper. Simmer for 5 minutes, then reduce the heat and taste to see if you need to adjust the seasoning. Keep tasting and adjusting until it reaches your desired level of savoriness.

Using a mesh spider or slotted spoon, gently place the wontons into the simmering soup and stir lightly. Cook the wontons over medium-high heat for 3 minutes or until they float to the top, then remove the soup from the heat. Serve the soup in bowls garnished with some more sesame oil or your favorite chili crisp, if desired, then finish with a sprinkle of reserved chopped scallions.

NOTE: *The vegetable filling requires a lot of chopping. You can use a food processor to work quickly and chop the vegetables into roughly ½-inch (1 cm) pieces, but don't allow them to be pureed.*

Silky Noodle Soup

PANCIT LOMI

Miki noodles, a type of thick and chewy wheat noodle, are perfect for slurping when simmered in a deeply flavorful soup. This recipe calls for chayote squash, which is a summer squash like zucchini—but with a similar texture to melon and just one big seed in the middle. You'll often find chayote at Asian supermarkets or the Asian or Latin vegetable section of your local grocer. The tofu puffs are spongy and pillowy, so they absorb a lot of flavor from the soup. Try this dish next time you're in the mood for something hearty but not too heavy.

SERVES 4 TO 6

- ¼ large (5 ounces/140 g) napa cabbage
- 1 large onion, peeled
- 4 garlic cloves, peeled
- 2 scallions, root ends trimmed off
- 1 large carrot, peeled
- 1 chayote squash (about ½ pound/226 g), peeled (or 1 zucchini)
- 1 tablespoon toasted sesame oil
- Kosher salt and black pepper
- 4½ cups (1,080 ml) water, boiled
- 2 tablespoons soy sauce
- 1½ teaspoons cornstarch
- 1 package (14 ounces/400 g) precooked plant-based miki noodles or udon
- 2 cups (160 g) tofu puffs

Place the cabbage on its base on a cutting board and slice it vertically into two halves. Lay the halves cut side down, trim off the base, and chop the cabbage leaves crosswise into ½-inch-thick (1 cm) slices. Set aside.

Chop the onion and set aside. Grate the garlic using a Microplane or grater into a small bowl. Chop the scallions, separate the whites from the greens, and set them aside in small bowls or ramekins.

Trim the root and stem ends off the carrot. Slice the carrot into ¼-inch-thick (6 mm) rounds. Working in batches, stack a few carrot slices and cut them into thin matchsticks. Set aside in yet another bowl.

Stand the chayote on its broad end on the cutting board and slice vertically in half between the ridges. Separate the two cheeks and scoop out the seed using a spoon. Working with one cheek at a time, place it on the cutting board with the flat side down. Cut it into ¼-inch-thick (6 mm) slices. Stack a few chayote slices at a time and slice them into thin matchsticks.

Add the sesame oil to a large saucepan and place over medium-high heat until the sesame oil is just warm. Add the onions to the oil and cook for 2 minutes or until translucent. Add the garlic and mix to combine. Quickly add the scallion whites, carrots, and chayote and season with a pinch of salt and about ¼ teaspoon of pepper. Stir and cook for 2 to 3 minutes, until the vegetables are glossy.

Add the water, reduce the heat to medium-low, and bring to a simmer. Add the soy sauce and stir to combine. Taste and adjust the seasoning if needed. Add the cabbage and stir to make sure everything is submerged in the water. Cover the pot with a lid and simmer for 3 to 4 minutes, until the cabbage is tender.

Combine the cornstarch and 1 tablespoon water in a small bowl to make a slurry. Add the slurry to the soup and gently mix for 1 minute to ensure the cornstarch doesn't clump up. At this point, feel free to add more water depending on how soupy you want the noodles to be. Stir and continue to simmer.

Add the noodles and gently stir to combine. Add the tofu puffs and stir again. Cover the pot and simmer for another 3 minutes to allow the flavors to come together. Serve the noodle soup in bowls with the scallion greens scattered over top.

Freestyle It

- You can replace the tofu puffs with **Multipurpose Tofu Crumbles** (page 45) for a crunchy texture. Add them at the very end just before serving the soup.

Dinners & Mains

Whether you're looking for a plant-based stir-fry or noodle dish, Filipino cuisine offers a treasure trove of recipes steeped in tradition. Easy enough for a casual weeknight dinner but pleasing enough to serve to guests, you can even make these dishes ahead to save yourself some time.

Stir-Fried Squash with Okra, Long Beans, and Eggplant

PINAKBET

This unassuming dish is a medley of vegetables stir-fried together in perfect harmony. It's an indigenous recipe that originated in the northern region of the Philippines. It comprises all the textures you want, from the tender squash and crunchy long beans to soft eggplant and slippery okra. If you can't stand the texture of okra, don't despair. You can skip it or add asparagus in its place, and this dish will still be delicious.

SERVES 4 TO 6

1 small kabocha or medium acorn squash (about 2 pounds/900 grams), well scrubbed

5 ounces (155 g) okra pods

1 bunch (5 ounces/150 g) long beans

1 large globe eggplant, or 2 Chinese eggplants (about 11 ounces/320 g total)

1 medium onion, peeled

4 garlic cloves, peeled

1 Roma tomato (about 2 ounces/60 g)

2 tablespoons vegetable oil

1 teaspoon kosher salt

½ teaspoon black pepper

6 tablespoons (90 ml) water

2 tablespoons soy sauce

1 scallion, trimmed and thinly sliced, for garnish

Stovetop Coconut and Lemongrass Rice (page 104) or steamed white rice (see page 103), for serving

Place the squash on a cutting board on its bottom (blossom end). Using a sharp chef's knife, pierce the squash across the top at the center, then carefully slice it in half with a rocking motion. Once you're halfway through, use your other hand to help push the knife down until the squash splits in half. Scoop out the seeds and fibers; discard them, or store in an airtight container to roast later. Place the flat, cut side down on the cutting board and cut the squash into 1-inch-thick (2.5 cm) wedges. If the stem or hard blossom end are still attached to the ends of wedges, cut them off. Chop the wedges into cubes. Set aside in a large mixing bowl.

Cut the stems off the okra pods, then chop the okra into ½-inch-thick (1 cm) rounds. Set aside. Align the bottom ends of the long beans and trim them off. Working in batches, slice the long beans into 3-inch (8 cm) pieces. Set them aside in a small bowl. Remove the eggplant stem and slice the eggplant into quarters lengthwise. Chop the quarters into 1-inch (2.5 cm) pieces; set aside in another bowl. Chop the onion and mince the garlic cloves. Set each aside in a small bowl or ramekin. Slice the tomato in half lengthwise, then chop into 1-inch (2.5 cm) pieces; do not remove the seeds.

Heat the oil in a large saucepan over medium-high heat. Cook the onions for 2 to 3 minutes, until translucent. Add the garlic and stir together until combined, then cook for about 1 minute. Add the tomatoes and season with a pinch of the salt; stir together and cook for 2 to 3 minutes, until the tomatoes are extra soft.

Add the squash and gently mix everything together. Cook for 5 minutes, stirring occasionally to ensure nothing sticks to the bottom of the pot. Add the okra and long beans and season with the remaining salt and the pepper. Stir together until combined. Add 2 tablespoons of the water. Cover with a lid and cook for 3 minutes or until the vegetables are heated through.

Add the eggplant, soy sauce, and the remaining 4 tablespoons (60 ml) water. Gently stir until combined. Reduce the heat to medium-low, cover, and cook for 10 to 12 minutes, until the vegetables are fork-tender. Taste and adjust the seasoning if needed. Remove from heat, garnish with sliced scallions, and serve with rice while hot.

Spicy Curried Taro Leaves

LAING

Taro is a root-like vegetable that looks similar to a potato. It's starchy, lightly sweet, and has a mild, nutty flavor. Its hearty, edible leaves taste similar to mustard greens and are as fibrous as kale. Spicy and creamy dishes like laing come from Bicol, a region of the Philippines known for its use of chiles and coconut milk.

SERVES 4 TO 6

- 1 pound (450 g) taro leaves
- 1 large taro or cassava (about 12 ounces/340 g)
- 5 garlic cloves, peeled
- 1 large onion, peeled
- 1 Thai red chile
- 1 tablespoon neutral oil such as vegetable, canola, or avocado
- 1½ teaspoons kosher salt
- ½ teaspoon black pepper
- 1 can (400 ml) coconut milk
- Stovetop Coconut and Lemongrass Rice (page 104) or steamed white rice (see page 103), for serving

Wash the taro leaves; dry them using a salad spinner or pat them dry with a clean kitchen towel. Chop the leaves into 1-inch (2.5 cm) pieces and set aside in a large mixing bowl.

Wash the taro and peel off the skin using a vegetable peeler. Slice the taro in half lengthwise. With the flat side down, cube into ½- to 1-inch (1 to 2 cm) pieces. Mince the garlic and chop the onion. Cut the stem off the chile. Slice the chile in half lengthwise; remove the seeds if you want less heat. Finely chop the chile. Set aside in a small bowl or ramekin.

(continued)

Heat the oil in a medium-large saucepan over medium heat. Add the onion, stir, and cook for 2 to 3 minutes, until translucent. Add the garlic, stir until combined, and cook for another minute. Add the taro and season with the salt and pepper; stir to combine. Cook for 3 to 4 minutes, stirring occasionally to prevent anything from sticking to the bottom of the pot, until the taro is heated through.

Add half of the chile and all of the taro leaves. Gently stir everything together until combined. Add the coconut milk and season with more salt and pepper. Stir again, cover the pot with a lid, and cook for 8 to 9 minutes, until the vegetables are fork-tender. Taste the sauce, add the remaining chile, and stir to combine. Adjust the seasoning as needed. Remove from heat and serve immediately with steamed rice.

Freestyle It

› Customize this dish by replacing the taro leaves with finely chopped kale, discarding the tough stems but keeping the small, tender ones. If you don't have red chiles, add 1 to 2 teaspoons of red pepper flakes or a generous amount of black pepper for spice.

Tofu and Green Bean Stir-Fry

GINISANG TOKWA'T SITAW

Simple tofu stir-fries taste better if you follow one trick: freeze the tofu overnight to improve its ability to absorb flavors and create a light and chewy texture. Freezing tofu causes its water molecules to expand and form ice crystals, changing the structure of the protein. When thawed with the water pressed out, the tofu is lighter and chewier in texture, which makes it perfect for stir-fries. Paired with green beans and tons of alliums, it makes a dish that will be a new weeknight staple.

SERVES 4 OR 5

- 1 block (14 ounces/400 g) extra firm tofu, frozen
- 11 ounces (330 g) green beans
- 5 garlic cloves, peeled
- 1 large red onion, peeled
- 4 scallions, root ends trimmed off
- 2 tablespoons neutral oil such as vegetable, canola, or avocado
- 1 teaspoon red pepper flakes
- 1 tablespoon soy sauce
- Kosher salt and black pepper
- Juice of ½ lime
- Sesame seeds, for garnish
- Stovetop Coconut and Lemongrass Rice (page 104) or steamed white rice (see page 103), for serving

If you're really planning ahead, move the package of frozen tofu to the refrigerator to thaw overnight. Or thaw the tofu on the countertop for 6 hours. If, however, you completely forgot to thaw the tofu earlier, simply transfer it from the package to a rimmed plate, then chuck it in the microwave for 10 minutes; let it cool for another 10 minutes before using it.

Drain the excess liquid from the tofu by gently pressing it down using a clean kitchen towel or paper towel against a cutting board. Wrap the tofu in the towel, then carefully squeeze more water out over the sink without breaking the block. Take your time in doing this to prevent the tofu from breaking apart. Clean the cutting board and place the tofu back on it.

(continued)

Slice the tofu down the middle from the top down then turn the halves 90 degrees and slice them into ½ inch (1 cm) pieces.

Place the green beans on the cutting board and align the tips evenly. Cut off and discard the tips and any stems. Thinly slice the garlic either lengthwise or crosswise, and set aside in a small bowl or ramekin. Slice the onion in half, then chop the halves. Cut the scallions into 3-inch (8 cm) pieces and separate the whites from the greens. Slice the green and white parts lengthwise into thin matchsticks and set aside separately.

Heat the oil in a nonstick, cast-iron, or stainless-steel skillet over medium-low heat. To check if the oil is hot enough, carefully place a small piece of tofu in the pan. If the oil bubbles around it, you're good to go. Place the tofu on its bigger surface in the pan in a single layer, making sure the pieces are not sticking to each other. (If your pan is too small, work in batches.) Fry the tofu for 4 to 5 minutes, then turn and cook another 4 to 5 minutes, until golden brown on both sides. Transfer to a plate and set aside.

Add the onions to the oil left in the pan and cook for 2 to 3 minutes, until translucent. Add the garlic and the scallion whites; stir together and cook for 2 minutes.

Add the green beans, season with the red pepper flakes, a pinch of salt, and about half a teaspoon of black pepper, and cook for another 5 to 6 minutes, until the green beans are fork-tender.

Add the fried tofu back into the pan along with the scallion greens and soy sauce and stir to combine. Taste and adjust the seasoning, then pour the lime juice over everything and stir again to combine. Remove from heat and garnish with sesame seeds; serve immediately with steamed rice.

Freestyle It

- Replace the green beans with 1 pound (450 g) of asparagus, trimmed and cut into 1-inch (2.5 cm) pieces. Cook for 6 to 7 minutes, or until the asparagus is fork-tender. Serve with a tablespoon of your favorite chili crisp for an extra kick.

Stir-Fried Bok Choy with Ground Tofu

GINISANG PECHAY AT TOKWA

This recipe embodies the fast and flexible nature of Filipino cooking. Bok choy is an inherently low-effort vegetable to cook because it takes no more than 10 minutes in the pan to soften. If you can't find bok choy, napa cabbage does the trick in the same amount of time. The ground tofu keeps this meal interesting with a crispy texture that turns satisfyingly chewy after you add soy sauce. Need a little more spice? Top it off with your favorite chili crisp for an extra kick.

SERVES 3 OR 4

Half of a 14-ounce (400 g) block extra firm tofu

1 pound (450 g) baby bok choy

1 large onion, peeled

4 garlic cloves, peeled

3 tablespoons neutral oil such as vegetable, canola, or avocado

1½ tablespoons soy sauce

Kosher salt and black pepper

1 teaspoon sesame seeds, for garnish

Stovetop Coconut and Lemongrass Rice (page 104) or steamed white rice (see page 103), for serving

Chili crisp, for serving

Wrap the tofu in a clean kitchen towel or paper towel and place it on a rimmed plate or shallow bowl. Top with a heavy item like a cutting board and a large can of beans or tomatoes; let sit for at least 30 minutes to press out excess water. Unwrap and pat dry. (Doing this will ensure your tofu can crisp up and absorb the seasoning easily.) Crumble the tofu into pea-sized pieces and set aside.

While the tofu is being pressed, wash the bok choy and pat it dry with a clean kitchen towel. Cut off and discard the ends of each bok choy, then rinse them again to remove any extra dirt from between the leaves. Set aside to drain well. Chop the onion and mince the garlic. Set each aside in a bowl or ramekin.

Heat 2 tablespoons of the oil in a large skillet over medium-high heat. Once the oil is hot, carefully spread the crumbled tofu across the bottom of the pan. Fry until it begins to crisp, 8 to 10 minutes. Sprinkle with 1 tablespoon of the soy sauce and toss together. Cook for another 5 minutes, stirring occasionally, until browned. Set aside in a bowl.

Pour the remaining 1 tablespoon oil into the same skillet and reduce the heat to medium-low. Add the onions and garlic, season with a pinch of salt, and cook for 2 to 3 minutes, until the onions are translucent. Add the bok choy, season with a pinch of salt and about half a teaspoon of pepper, and cook for 2 minutes or until the stalks are translucent. Add the remaining soy sauce, stir to thoroughly combine, and cook for another 4 to 5 minutes, until the bok choy is tender.

Add the cooked tofu back into the skillet and gently combine everything together. Taste and adjust the seasoning with more salt and pepper if needed. Transfer to a serving plate and garnish with sesame seeds. Serve immediately with steamed rice and chili crisp.

Freestyle It

- You can replace the baby bok choy with 1 pound of either yu choy or Chinese broccoli. The stalks will be thicker, so be sure to cook it for an extra 5 to 6 minutes or until tender.

Bok Choy Adobo

ADOBONG PECHAY

Adobo could be called the mascot of Filipino cuisine. A delicious Filipino adobo marries the fundamental flavors that have come to define the cuisine throughout its complex history: sweet, salty, tangy, and *very* garlicky. The bok choy's tender and thin leaves readily wilt and soften as soon as they're exposed to heat, making this dish come together in almost no time. As it simmers in the adobo sauce, the bok choy becomes tender and succulent. Serve with steamed rice, and top off with sesame seeds for extra texture.

SERVES 2 OR 3

1 pound (450 g) baby bok choy

7 garlic cloves, peeled

1 large onion, peeled

1 teaspoon neutral oil such as vegetable, canola, or avocado

1 cup (240 ml) water

¼ cup (60 ml) soy sauce

¼ cup (55 g) packed brown sugar

1½ tablespoons cane vinegar, plus more if needed

4 dried bay leaves

Kosher salt and black pepper

Sesame seeds, for serving

Stovetop Coconut and Lemongrass Rice (page 104) or steamed white rice (see page 103), for serving

Wash the bok choy and pat dry with a clean kitchen towel. Cut off and discard the base of each bunch of bok choy. Rinse the bok choy again to remove any extra dirt from between the leaves. Set aside to drain well.

Chop the garlic. Slice the onion in half vertically, then slice each half into half-moons.

Heat the oil in a medium saucepan over medium heat. Add the onions and garlic and cook for 2 to 3 minutes, until translucent. Add the water, soy sauce, brown sugar, vinegar, and bay leaves, and stir to combine. Simmer for 3 minutes or until slightly reduced.

(continued)

Add the bok choy, season with salt and pepper, and gently mix to combine. Cover the pan and reduce the heat to medium-low. Simmer for 5 to 6 minutes, until the bok choy is tender. Remove from heat, take out and discard the bay leaves, and sprinkle with sesame seeds. Serve immediately with steamed rice.

Freestyle It

- You can replace the baby bok choy with 1 pound of either yu choy or Chinese broccoli. The stalks will be thicker, so be sure to cook it for an extra 5 to 6 minutes or until tender. Serve as a side to **Steamed Mushroom Buns** (page 133).

Roasted Mushrooms with Sticky Adobo Sauce

This version of mushroom adobo is a modern take on the traditional dish. The mushrooms end up charred and golden brown instead of braised, thanks to the power of roasting (for tips on cooking with mushrooms, see page 98). Using the same ingredients as a traditional adobo recipe, the sauce offers the original sweet and tart flavors. It's perfect with a bowl of steamed rice, but can also be served with a crunchy salad.

SERVES 2 TO 4

7 garlic cloves, peeled

1 large onion, peeled

2 scallions, root ends trimmed off

1 tablespoon cornstarch

1 cup (240 ml) water

1 pound (455 g) oyster mushrooms, cleaned (see page 98)

3 tablespoons neutral oil such as vegetable, canola, or avocado

¼ cup (60 ml) soy sauce

¼ cup (55 g) packed brown sugar

1½ tablespoons cane vinegar, plus more if needed

4 dried bay leaves

Kosher salt and black pepper

Stovetop Coconut and Lemongrass Rice (page 104) or steamed white rice (see page 103), for serving

Preheat the oven to 400°F (205°C). Line two rimmed baking sheets with parchment paper.

Thinly slice the garlic either lengthwise or crosswise. Set aside in a small bowl or ramekin. Slice the onion in half vertically, then slice each half into half-moons; set aside. Slice the scallions into thin rounds and set aside.

Combine the cornstarch with 1 tablespoon of the water in a small bowl and whisk until smooth.

(continued)

Gently break the mushrooms apart into large, flat pieces and place them on the baking sheets, making sure to spread them evenly and not overcrowd each pan. Drizzle the mushrooms with 2 tablespoons of the oil and gently toss them using your hands. Spread them out again. Roast for 25 to 30 minutes, until golden brown.

While the mushrooms are roasting, heat the remaining 1 tablespoon oil in a saucepan over medium heat. Add the onions and garlic and cook for 2 minutes or until translucent and tender. Add the soy sauce, brown sugar, vinegar, bay leaves, the rest of the water, a pinch of salt, and about half a teaspoon of pepper, and whisk to combine. Bring to a simmer for 4 to 5 minutes to bring the flavors together and dissolve the sugar. Add the cornstarch slurry, whisk until smooth, and bring back to a simmer. Remove from heat once the sauce has thickened. Take out and discard the bay leaves.

Take the oyster mushrooms out of the oven and sprinkle lightly with salt while they're still hot. Let them cool for about 5 minutes, then gently toss them using your hands to season evenly. Serve the roasted mushrooms with a few spoonfuls of the sauce on top. Add more pepper, if you like, and garnish with the scallions. Serve immediately with steamed rice.

Meal-ify It

- Serve the mushrooms in a grain bowl using brown rice, quinoa, or couscous. Drizzle with some more of the sauce, your favorite chili crisp, and a sprinkle of toasted sesame seeds for a spicy and nutty bite.

The Best Way to Sear Mushrooms

All it takes are a few simple steps to upgrade any plant-based dish with seared mushrooms.

CLEANING MUSHROOMS

Don't let dirt spoil the taste of your mushrooms. Use a dry kitchen towel or paper towel to gently wipe every nook and cranny. If you find something that's too difficult to wipe off, you can use a pastry brush with natural bristles to remove the dirt. Keeping the mushrooms dry will help them crisp up nicely and ensure they get a deep golden color rather than turning gray.

If, however, the mushrooms won't get clean unless you wash them with water, there is a way forward without sacrificing the mushrooms' texture. A mistake people often make when washing mushrooms is *soaking* them in water—if this is you, stop immediately! Unless you want soggy and ugly mushrooms, you should not be soaking them in water. Mushrooms are as absorbent as sponges. If you plan on using water to clean your mushrooms, know that leaving them for too long could make them slimy, so work as quickly as you can.

The key to washing mushrooms *correctly* is to toss them in a bowl of water for 40 seconds to 1 minute, lift them out of the water, and immediately pat them dry with a paper towel or kitchen towel. As soon as they're dry, check for any remaining dirt and remove it with another dry towel, paper towel, or pastry brush.

SEARING MUSHROOMS

Use a large, heavy-bottomed skillet, such as a cast-iron or stainless-steel pan, with enough surface area to spread out the mushrooms in a single layer. If you're working with a smaller pan, cook in batches to avoid overcrowding. If placed too close together, the mushrooms will release their water and steam, ruining the searing process and preventing them from achieving that beautiful golden brown color and crispy texture you're looking for.

Before placing the mushrooms into the pan, make sure they're completely dry. Any moisture can cause the oil to splatter. Heat the oil until it's shimmering hot, but not yet smoking. The heat should be set to medium-high, but use your intuition and reduce the heat or remove the pan from the stovetop for a moment if it gets too hot.

Once you place the mushrooms in the pan, avoid the temptation to salt them. Salting too early can draw out moisture, which will set back the crispy texture you're working so hard to create. Instead, cook the mushrooms undisturbed for 2 to 3 minutes, until golden brown on the bottom, then flip them over to cook the other side. Wait to salt them until halfway through cooking, when one side is already golden brown.

Sizzling Mushroom and Tofu Sisig

Sisig is a popular pan-fried side dish or appetizer with an irresistibly crispy and chewy bite. Its origins lie in the use of excess meat from the commissaries of American military facilities in the Philippines, where Filipinos learned to be frugal and avoid food waste. In this plant-based version, using potato starch to coat the mushrooms is the key to achieving a super-crispy yet chewy texture. To experience sisig to its full effect, eat it over a bed of rice with a pint of cold beer or any fizzy beverage.

SERVES 2 TO 4

Half of a 14-ounce (400 g) block extra firm tofu

5 garlic cloves, peeled

1 medium red onion or 2 shallots, peeled

2 scallions, root ends trimmed off

2 red chile peppers

1 pound (455 g) oyster mushrooms or shiitake mushroom caps

½ cup (75 g) potato starch or (60 g) rice flour

½ cup (120 ml) neutral oil such as vegetable, canola, or avocado

Kosher salt

2½ tablespoons soy sauce

1 tablespoon vegan mayonnaise

½ lime, for serving

Stovetop Coconut and Lemongrass Rice (page 104) or steamed white rice (see page 103), for serving

Wrap the tofu in a clean kitchen towel or paper towel and place it on a rimmed plate or shallow bowl. Top with a heavy item like a cutting board and a large can of beans or tomatoes; let sit for at least 30 minutes to press out excess water. Unwrap and pat dry. Crumble the tofu into pea-sized pieces.

Meanwhile, thinly slice the garlic either lengthwise or crosswise. Dice the onion. Slice the scallions into ½- to 1-inch-thick (1 to 2 cm) rounds and set aside to use for garnish. Cut the stems off the chiles. Slice the chiles in half

(continued)

lengthwise; remove the seeds if you want less heat. Chop the chiles and set aside.

If using oyster mushrooms, gently break them apart into large, flat pieces. Clean the mushrooms as directed on page 98. Place them in a large mixing bowl. Sprinkle with the potato starch and gently toss together using your hands.

Heat a large cast-iron skillet over medium-high heat. To check if it's hot enough, add a drop of water; if you see the water dancing around, let it evaporate, then pour in ¼ cup (60 ml) of the oil. Working in batches, gently place the mushrooms in the pan in a single layer, making sure they're not sticking to each other. Fry for 6 to 7 minutes on each side, until golden brown and crispy. Remove from heat and transfer to a cutting board to cool. Chop the fried mushrooms into ½- to 1-inch (1 to 2 cm) pieces and set aside.

In the meantime, heat the remaining ¼ cup (60 ml) oil in a skillet or wok over medium-high heat (see Note). Once the oil is shimmering hot, add the crumbled tofu, making sure it's spread out evenly. Fry the tofu until it starts to crisp up, 8 to 10 minutes, then toss to let the other side crisp up for another 10 minutes. Remove from heat, transfer to a clean bowl, season with salt, and toss.

Return the same cast-iron skillet to the stovetop over medium heat, add the onions and garlic, and cook for 2 minutes or until translucent. Add the cooked tofu and mushrooms and stir to combine. Add the chiles, soy sauce, mayonnaise, and about a teaspoon of salt and stir together until evenly mixed. Fry together for another 3 to 4 minutes, stirring occasionally, until the mayonnaise has been fully incorporated. Serve directly from the skillet, garnished with the scallions and a squeeze of lime juice. Serve with steamed rice.

NOTE: *I recommend using two skillets to save time while frying the mushrooms and tofu, but feel free to use just one skillet and reuse the frying oil. To get the full sizzling-plate experience, you can also make this sisig in a cast-iron skillet and serve it directly from the hot skillet. Place a wooden trivet under the skillet to protect your table and your hands.*

EVERYDAY STEAMED WHITE RICE

A bowl of hot and fluffy white rice is the ideal companion to savory main dishes. Its neutral taste serves as a canvas for the rich and diverse flavors in Filipino cuisine, allowing each dish to shine without overwhelming the palate.

To cook perfect steamed white rice, use jasmine or Calrose, which have a distinctly plumper texture than basmati. Before cooking, be sure to rinse the grains in a fine-mesh strainer until the water runs clear. This helps remove excess surface starch and prevents the steamed rice from clumping together.

Using a 1:1 ratio of water to rice (by volume) is the easiest way to cook rice without having to constantly check the pot. For best results, use a rice cooker, which will immediately stop cooking as soon as the rice is ready and keep the rice warm until you're ready to eat. If you don't own a rice cooker, cook the rice in a medium saucepan over medium heat for 12 to 15 minutes, until the rice is soft and fluffy. Serve immediately, while hot. Store any leftovers in an airtight container in the refrigerator for up to 4 days.

Stovetop Coconut and Lemongrass Rice

The humble pot of steamed white rice benefits greatly from the addition of a few aromatic ingredients. Creamy coconut milk leaves the rice tasting buttery and nutty, while the lemongrass infuses a citrusy fragrance throughout every grain. Pair this flavorful rice with any savory dish to complete a meal, and turn leftovers into Garlic Fried Rice (page 21).

SERVES 3 OR 4

3 cups (580 g) jasmine rice
2 lemongrass stalks
1 can (400 ml) coconut milk
1 cup (240 ml) water
Pinch of kosher salt

Rinse the rice 2 or 3 times in a fine-mesh strainer under cold water until the water runs clear. Transfer it to a heavy-bottomed saucepan with a lid.

Trim off the root end and the tough outer leaves from the lemongrass until you reach the white part. Slice the lemongrass into 3-inch-long (8 cm) slivers.

Add the coconut milk, water, lemongrass, and salt to the rice, stir to combine, and place over medium heat. Cover the saucepan with its lid. Cook for 12 minutes or until the rice is tender. If liquid seeps out from under the lid, reduce the heat to low and slide the lid to the side, leaving just enough space for steam to escape.

Remove the lid, allowing the liquid to cook off for another 2 to 3 minutes.

Remove from heat and serve immediately.

Store any leftovers in an airtight container in the refrigerator for up to 2 days.

Meal-ify It

- Serve with **Sizzling Mushroom and Tofu Sisig** (page 101) or any soup, stew, or stir-fry.

FRANCE

Arroz a la Valenciana

Arroz a la Valenciana, often dubbed "the poor man's paella," was introduced to the Philippines by Spanish settlers during the colonial era, and has since been adapted by Filipinos as their own. What sets the Filipino version apart from the original is the use of glutinous rice and coconut milk, making each bite satisfyingly sticky and fragrant. The rice develops a yellow hue and subtle smoky flavor from the addition of annatto powder, which you can find in the international aisle of most grocery stores. Bring a pot of this to your next potluck, and you're guaranteed to introduce folks to their new favorite rice dish.

SERVES 4 TO 6

1 cup (195 g) white rice such as jasmine or Calrose

1 cup (195 g) glutinous rice

1 large onion, peeled

5 garlic cloves, peeled

1 red bell pepper

1 green bell pepper

1 bunch (about 55 g) parsley, stems included

2 tablespoons neutral oil such as vegetable, grapeseed, or avocado

2 tablespoons tomato paste

1 tablespoon annatto powder

Kosher salt and black pepper

1 can (400 ml) coconut milk

2 cups (500 ml) vegetable broth

½ cup (70 g) green peas (fresh or frozen)

Rinse the white rice 2 or 3 times in a fine-mesh strainer under cold water until the water runs clear. Drain well and set aside in a large bowl. Repeat with the glutinous rice and add to the same bowl.

Chop the onion and mince the garlic. Slice the tops off the bell peppers and pull off the stems. Slice the peppers in half lengthwise and remove the white membranes and seeds using a paring knife. Slice the peppers into thin vertical pieces. Transfer to another bowl. Chop the parsley (stems included) and set aside.

(continued)

Heat the oil in a large heavy-bottomed pot over medium-high heat for about 1 minute, until shimmering. Add the onions and cook for 2 minutes or until translucent. Add the garlic and cook for another 2 minutes. Add the rices, tomato paste, annatto powder, and a large pinch each of salt and pepper. Stir for 2 minutes or until everything is combined and the seasoning is fragrant. Pour in the coconut milk and vegetable broth and stir to combine. Add the green peas and bell peppers and season with another pinch of salt and pepper. Stir to evenly distribute the vegetables. Cover the pot and reduce the heat to medium. Simmer for 35 to 40 minutes, stirring every 10 minutes to prevent the rice from sticking to the bottom of the pot, until tender and sticky.

Taste the rice and adjust the seasoning with more salt and pepper if needed, making sure to stir them in well as you add them. When the rice is cooked through, remove from heat, garnish with parsley, and serve while hot.

Freestyle It

- Spice up your **Arroz a la Valenciana** by topping it with **Multipurpose Tofu Crumbles** (page 45) seasoned with paprika, chili powder, garlic powder, onion powder, dried oregano, salt, and pepper. You can also add **Crunchy Garlic Chips** (page 49) for added texture.

Vegetable Stir-Fried Noodles

PANCIT GUISADO

Inspired by Chinese longevity noodles, these stir-fried noodles are a representation of long life in the Philippines, which is why you'll often find them served at birthday parties. They look as vibrant as they taste, adorned with a variety of colorful vegetables and flavored with a blend of savory soy sauce, sesame oil, and MSG. Each bite is light and chewy, and has the perfect vegetable-to-noodle ratio. You can find Golden Bihon noodles next to the rice noodles at your local Asian market, but if you can't get your hands on them, feel free to opt for thin rice noodles instead.

SERVES 2 TO 4

- Kosher salt and pepper
- 4 ounces (110 g) green beans
- 6 napa cabbage leaves
- 1 large carrot, peeled
- 1 lime
- 3 garlic cloves, peeled
- 1 large onion, peeled
- 1 scallion, root ends trimmed off
- 1 package (16 ounces/454 g) cornstarch-based noodles (look for Super Q brand Golden Bihon or Special Palabok)
- 2 tablespoons neutral oil such as vegetable, grapeseed, or avocado
- 6½ tablespoons (96 ml) soy sauce
- 3 tablespoons toasted sesame oil
- 2 teaspoons MSG (optional)

Bring a large pot of water to a boil and season it with salt.

Remove the stems from the green beans, then thinly slice them on a bias. Stack the cabbage leaves together and chop them into thin ribbons. Slice the carrot on the bias about ¼ inch thick (6 mm); working in batches, stack a few carrot slices and slice into matchsticks. Slice the lime into wedges. Chop the garlic, onion, and scallions. Set everything aside.

Cook the noodles in the boiling water for 3 to 4 minutes, until tender. Remove the pot from the heat and drain the noodles. Return the noodles

(continued)

to the pot and immediately fill it with cold water, moving the noodles around with your hands to remove excess starch and ensure they won't stick together. Drain the noodles through the sieve again, then use a pair of kitchen shears to make a few cuts to the noodles to make them easier to eat. Set aside.

Heat a large wok or heavy-bottomed skillet over medium-high heat for 2 to 3 minutes, until warm, and then add the neutral oil. Add the onions and garlic and season with a pinch of salt. Cook for 2 to 3 minutes, until softened. Add the carrots and green beans, season with more salt and a pinch of pepper, and cook for another 4 to 5 minutes, stirring occasionally, until glossy and vibrant. Add the cabbage, season with another pinch of salt, and stir together to combine.

Add the cooked noodles and stir gently until the vegetables and noodles are fully mixed. Season with the soy sauce, sesame oil, MSG (if using), and salt and pepper to taste. Cook, tossing occasionally, for another 10 to 12 minutes, until fully combined. Taste the noodles and adjust the seasoning if needed. Once you're happy with the flavor, remove from heat and serve with the scallions scattered on top.

Freestyle It

- Substitute the cornstarch-based noodles with either sotanghon (vermicelli), rice noodles, canton, or chow mein. You can also add 3 tablespoons of plant-based oyster sauce and a cornstarch slurry made with 1 teaspoon of cornstarch and 2 teaspoons of water (mixed until smooth) for a saucier finish.

Noodles in Annatto Gravy

PALABOK

Annatto powder is a mildly sweet and nutty spice that tastes like paprika and turmeric combined. This fragrant seasoning gives the sauce its deep orange color and light, peppery taste. Similar to a slow-cooked ragù, pour this sauce on top of the cooked noodles and add other toppings just before serving.

SERVES 4 TO 6

- 1 large onion, peeled
- 4 garlic cloves, peeled
- 2 tablespoons cornstarch
- 3½ cups (840 ml) water
- 2 scallions, root ends trimmed off
- 1 lime
- 2 teaspoons toasted sesame oil
- Kosher salt and pepper
- 1 vegetable bouillon cube
- 1½ tablespoons annatto powder
- 1 tablespoon soy sauce
- 1 package (16 ounces/454 g) cornstarch-based noodles (look for Super Q brand Golden Bihon or Special Palabok)
- ¼ cup (65 g) Multipurpose Tofu Crumbles (page 45)
- 2 tablespoons Crunchy Garlic Chips (page 49)

Dice the onion into ¼-inch (6 mm) pieces. Mince the garlic. Combine the cornstarch with 2 tablespoons of the water in a small bowl and stir until fully dissolved to make a slurry. Chop the scallions into thin rounds. Slice the lime into wedges.

Heat a large saucepan over medium-high heat for about 30 seconds to 1 minute. Add the sesame oil and swirl it around by tilting the pan. Add the onions and garlic, season with a pinch of salt, and stir. Cook for 2 to 3 minutes, until the edges have browned a little bit, but not to the point where the onions are burnt. Add the remaining water, then bring to a boil. Reduce the heat to medium-low. Add the bouillon cube, annatto powder, soy sauce, salt, and pepper and stir to combine. Add the slurry and stir constantly for about a minute or two to incorporate it into the sauce.

Simmer for 3 to 5 minutes, stirring every couple of minutes to prevent clumps, until the sauce thickens. The texture of the sauce should be thick and cohesive, with no clumps. Taste and adjust the seasoning as needed. Reduce the heat to low and keep it on low until you're ready to serve, stirring occasionally to prevent the sauce from sticking.

Bring another large pot of water to a boil. Add the noodles to cook 4 to 5 minutes, until tender. Drain the noodles and rinse them under cold water, using your hands to separate them from each other. Drain again, then cut using kitchen shears to make them easier to serve.

Transfer the cooked noodles into a large serving bowl and pour the sauce over the top, making sure it's evenly dispersed. Top with the scallions, tofu crumbles, and garlic chips. Serve hot, with the lime wedges for squeezing over.

Vegetable Spring Rolls

LUMPIANG GULAY

Every Filipino mom likely has her own recipe for lumpiang gulay, and while nothing beats a mother's cooking, this take on the Filipino fan favorite food comes close. The best lumpia are crispy on the outside and filled with tender vegetables and tofu on the inside. You can't go wrong pairing them with banana ketchup, your choice of store-bought sweet chili sauce, or Daily Dipping Sauce (page 48). Lumpia are real crowd pleasers. Make them ahead and keep them stored in a heavy resealable bag in the freezer for up to 1 month to be ready to fry any time. Be sure to thaw them for about 30 minutes before frying.

MAKES 15 TO 20 LUMPIA

9 ounces (260 g) extra firm tofu (about ⅔ of a 14-ounce/400 g block)

1 medium white onion, peeled

1 large carrot, peeled

4 ounces (110 g) green beans, trimmed

1 cup (90 g) bean sprouts

1½ teaspoons kosher salt

1 package (16 ounces/454 g) 8 × 8-inch (20 × 20 cm) spring roll wrappers, thawed if frozen

2 cups (480 ml) neutral oil such as vegetable, grapeseed, or avocado, for frying

Sweet chili sauce or banana ketchup, for serving (optional)

Wrap the tofu in a clean kitchen towel or paper towel and place it on a rimmed plate or shallow bowl. Top with a heavy item like a cutting board and a large can of beans or tomatoes; let sit for at least 30 minutes to press out excess water. Unwrap and pat dry. Slice the tofu into ½-inch-thick (1 cm) sticks, about 2 inches (5 cm) long; set aside on a plate.

Slice the onion in half vertically, then slice each half into thin half-moons. Slice the carrot into 3-inch-long (8 cm) sections, then cut each section into matchsticks. Slice the green beans on the bias about ¼-inch thick (6 mm). Transfer all the vegetables to a large mixing bowl and add the bean sprouts. Season with the salt and mix thoroughly.

(continued)

To assemble the lumpia, follow the guide on page 117. Use 2 pieces of the tofu and 1 to 2 tablespoons of the vegetable filling for each lumpia. (If you have any wrappers left, wrap the package well in plastic or put it in a heavy resealable bag or airtight container, and put them back in the freezer for another time.)

Once you've rolled all the lumpia, transfer them to a heavy resealable bag or airtight container and freeze for about 1 hour, to firm them up.

When you're ready to cook, remove as many lumpia from the freezer as you need and fry them immediately. (Keep any extras in the freezer for up to a month until you need them. Thaw frozen lumpia at room temperature for 30 minutes before frying.)

Fit a wire rack inside a rimmed baking sheet. Heat the oil in a large heavy-bottomed skillet over medium-high heat. Drop in a small piece of a wrapper to make sure the oil is hot enough for frying; the oil will bubble around it once it's ready. Alternatively, you can use a wooden chopstick to check; bubbles should form around the end when it is inserted in the oil.

Gently place 5 or 6 lumpia (or as many as you can fit) seam side down in the skillet, making sure they don't stick to each other. Fry on one side for 2 to 3 minutes, until golden brown, then flip and fry the other side. Reduce the heat to medium-low if the lumpia seem to be browning too quickly. Transfer the cooked lumpia with tongs to the wire rack to drain. Continue to fry in batches. Serve the lumpia hot with sweet chili sauce or banana ketchup, if desired.

Meal-ify It

- Serve the lumpia with **Vegetable Stir-Fried Noodles** (page 109) and **Tangy Pickled Papaya** (page 43) for a well-rounded, vegetable-packed meal.

A GUIDE TO ROLLING LUMPIA

Prepare a cup of water for sealing the lumpia.

Separate a wrapper from the stack by using your thumb to lift one of the corners. Then with your index finger, pinch the corner and gently peel off the wrapper. Cover the stack of wrappers with a kitchen towel to prevent them from drying out.

Place a single wrapper on a clean work surface or cutting board with a corner facing you—it should look like a diamond. Add the filling 1 to 2 inches (2.5 to 5 cm) above the bottom corner, then spread it across into a log, leaving 1 to 2 inches (2.5 to 5 cm) empty on the left and right corners of the wrapper.

Working from the bottom, fold the wrapper up and over the filling, and tuck the bottom corner underneath the filling.

Fold in the left and right sides, then roll it up from the bottom until you have only about an inch (2.5 cm) of the wrapper left uncovered at the top.

Dip your finger in the water and run it along the exposed top corner of the wrapper, then continue to roll up until it seals.

Transfer the lumpia to a baking sheet with the seam side down to secure the seal.

Now you're a pro.

Using 8 × 8-inch (20 × 20 cm) spring roll wrappers gives you enough wiggle room for folding. If you can't find this size, you're welcome to use any size, but make sure to adjust the amount of filling you use so you don't overfill the wrapper.

Fresh Spring Rolls

LUMPIANG SARIWA

This spring roll uses fresh wrappers with a crepe-like texture and is filled with a mix of tender vegetables and tofu. Served with a peanut sauce, this lumpia balances the creamy peanut butter with sweet brown sugar and salty soy sauce.

MAKES 12 TO 15 LUMPIA

FILLING

9 ounces (260 g) extra firm tofu (about ⅔ of a 14-ounce/400 g block)

1 medium white onion, peeled

3 large garlic cloves, peeled

1 large carrot, peeled

1 medium yellow potato (about 8 ounces/225 g), peeled

1 tablespoons neutral oil such as vegetable, grapeseed, or avocado

Kosher salt and black pepper

WRAPPERS

1 cup (125 g) all-purpose flour

¼ cup (30 g) cornstarch

1½ teaspoons kosher salt

1½ cups (360 ml) unsweetened plant-based milk such as oat, almond, or soy

3 tablespoons neutral oil such as vegetable, grapeseed, or avocado, plus more for cooking

SAUCE

⅔ cup (160 ml) soy sauce

1 cup (220 g) packed brown sugar

2 tablespoons peanut butter

4 cups (960 ml) water

4 tablespoons cornstarch

1 cup (75 g) peanuts, chopped

Kosher salt and black pepper

1 head green leaf lettuce, leaves separated, rinsed well, and dried, for serving

Wrap the tofu in a clean kitchen towel or paper towel and place it on a rimmed plate or shallow bowl. Top with a heavy item like a cutting board and a large can of beans or tomatoes; let sit for at least 30 minutes to press out excess water. Unwrap and pat dry. Slice the tofu into ½-inch-thick (1 cm) sticks, about 2 inches (5 cm) long; set aside on a plate.

(continued)

Slice the onion in half vertically, then slice each half into thin half-moons. Mince the garlic. Slice the carrot and potato into 3-inch-long (8 cm) matchsticks. Set aside.

To make the wrappers, whisk together the flour, cornstarch, and salt in a medium mixing bowl. Slowly add the milk and 3 tablespoons oil and whisk until smooth.

Pour in just enough oil to cover the surface of a 12-inch (30 cm) skillet and place it over medium-low heat. Using a small piece of paper towel, spread the oil around the pan evenly. Once the oil is hot, pour in ¼ cup (60 ml) of the batter and quickly spread it around the pan with the back of a spoon until you have a paper-thin round crepe. Cook the first side for 2 to 3 minutes, until the edges are looking dry. Flip and cook another 2 to 3 minutes, until the wrapper is cooked through and can be easily removed. The wrappers should be soft and not browned. Transfer the cooked wrappers to a plate to cool; it's okay if you pile them on top of each other. Repeat until all the batter is used, spreading oil around the pan using a small piece of paper towel each time.

To cook the filling, heat the oil in a large skillet over medium-high heat. Add the onions and garlic and cook for 2 to 3 minutes, until tender. Add the potatoes, stir to combine, and fry for 4 to 5 minutes, until the edges start to soften. Add the carrots and season with a pinch of salt. Stir thoroughly and cook for another 5 to 6 minutes, until the potatoes are slightly tender. Add the tofu, season with another pinch of salt and a pinch of pepper, and mix until combined. Cook for another 7 minutes, or until vegetables are tender. Remove from heat and set aside.

To make the sauce, combine the soy sauce, brown sugar, and peanut butter in a saucepan and whisk well. Place the saucepan over medium-low heat. Combine the water and cornstarch in a bowl and whisk until smooth. Pour the cornstarch slurry into the saucepan and quickly whisk together. Add a pinch each of salt and pepper and continue to whisk. As the sauce starts to thicken, add half of the peanuts and mix until combined. Simmer for another 6 to 7 minutes, until the sauce thickens, whisking occasionally to ensure the sauce doesn't have clumps. Keep warm.

To assemble the lumpia, place a wrapper on a clean surface. Add a lettuce leaf on top of the wrapper and add 2 to 3 tablespoons of the filling down the center, leaving 1 to 2 inches (2.5 to 5 cm) empty space on each side of the filling. Fold in the left and right sides of the wrapper, then roll it up tightly from the bottom. Transfer the lumpia to a large serving plate with the seam side down. Repeat until you've used up all of the wrappers and filling.

To serve, pour 3 to 4 heaping tablespoons of the sauce over each lumpia and top with the remainder of the peanuts. Serve immediately.

Snacks

Crunchy, salty snacks go far beyond a bowl of chips when it comes to Filipino food. Savory fritters and satisfying spring rolls are perfect to serve at a party, as an appetizer, or for an afternoon snack.

Crunchy Vegetable Fritters

OKOY

These fritters are a great way to make use of any vegetables you have lying around your fridge before they go to waste. Traditionally, okoy is made with small shrimp, but replacing the shrimp with a variety of vegetables keeps the fritters interesting every time you choose to make them. Crispy on the outside and tender on the inside, each fritter is a treat served with a spicy dipping sauce.

MAKES 12 TO 15 FRITTERS; SERVES 4 TO 6

FRITTERS

2 sweet potatoes, peeled, or 1 kabocha squash (about 2 pounds/900 grams)

1 large carrot, peeled

1 large red onion, peeled

1 bunch chives

2 cups (180 g) bean sprouts

Kosher salt

1 cup (125 g) all-purpose flour

½ cup (65 g) cornstarch

1 teaspoon annatto powder

1¼ cups (300 ml) water

Neutral oil such as vegetable, grapeseed, or avocado, for frying

DIPPING SAUCE

1 Thai red chile

1 shallot or ¼ red onion, peeled

½ cup (120 ml) cane vinegar

1 teaspoon soy sauce

Kosher salt and black pepper

Shred the sweet potatoes on the large holes of a box grater. If using kabocha squash, peel the skin, then slice the squash in half and remove the seeds. Shred the squash on the large holes of a box grater. Shred the carrot on the large holes of a box grater. Slice the onion in half vertically, then slice each half into thin half-moons. Using kitchen shears, cut the chives into 3-inch (8 cm) pieces. Combine everything in a large mixing bowl with the bean sprouts and season with about ½ teaspoon of salt. Mix well. Let sit for 20 to 25 minutes to expel the excess water.

(continued)

Meanwhile, make the dipping sauce: Cut the stem off the chile. Slice the chile in half lengthwise; remove the seeds if you want less heat. Finely chop the chile and the shallot and place in a small bowl. Add the vinegar, soy sauce, a pinch of salt, and about a quarter teaspoon of pepper, and stir to combine. Taste and adjust the seasoning if necessary. Set aside until you're ready to serve.

Combine the all-purpose flour, cornstarch, annatto powder, and water in another large mixing bowl and whisk together. Squeeze the vegetables and drain the excess water. Transfer the vegetables to the batter. Add a large pinch of salt and mix to ensure all the vegetable strands are coated with batter.

Line a rimmed baking sheet with paper towels and fit a wire rack inside.

Fill a heavy-bottomed skillet or wok with about ¼ inch (6 mm) oil, just enough to cover the surface for a shallow fry. Place the skillet over medium heat. Check if the oil is hot enough by adding a small drop of batter. If the oil bubbles around it, you can start cooking. Scoop up 2 to 3 tablespoons of the fritter mixture using a ladle or stainless-steel spoon and drop it into the hot oil. Use the bottom of the ladle or back of the spoon to flatten the fritter slightly and form it into an even round. Repeat to make 2 or 3 fritters at a time and fry them for 4 to 5 minutes on each side, until golden brown, making sure they don't stick to each other.

Remove the cooked fritters from the oil using a mesh spider or stainless-steel slotted spoon, and transfer them to the wire rack to briefly drain any excess oil. Cook as many fritters as you need. Serve the fritters hot with the dipping sauce. Store any leftover batter in the refrigerator for 1 day.

Garlicky Fried Peanuts

ADOBONG MANI

Level up your late-night snack game by pairing these easy and addicting fried peanuts with an ice-cold drink. The fried shallots aren't traditional, but will take these nuts over the top with added crispness and caramelized sweetness. Be sure to season the peanuts while they're hot, so the salt sticks to them.

SERVES 4 TO 6

1 shallot, peeled

1 bulb garlic, papery outer skin removed

2 cups (480 ml) neutral oil such as vegetable, grapeseed, or avocado, for frying

1 pound (455 g) raw red-skinned peanuts

Kosher salt

Slice the shallot into paper-thin rounds. (Use a mandoline for this step if you have one.) Separate the shallot slices into rings. Separate each garlic clove from the bulb and gently crush each one using the flat side of a chef's knife. Peel off the skin and thinly slice each clove crosswise.

Add the oil to a wok or large heavy-bottomed skillet and place it over medium-high heat. Use a deep-fry thermometer to check the temperature of the oil, maintaining it at 350°F (175°C). Line a large mixing bowl and a plate with paper towels.

Gently place the shallot rings in the wok and fry them for 3 to 4 minutes, until golden brown, stirring occasionally for even color. Remove the shallots using a fine-mesh strainer or mesh spider and spread them on the paper towel–lined plate to drain off the excess oil.

Reduce the heat to medium-low. When the oil temperature reaches 325°F (160°C), fry the garlic for 3 to 4 minutes, until medium brown, stirring

(continued)

occasionally for an even color and to prevent the garlic from burning. Transfer the garlic to the same plate as the fried shallots to drain.

In the same oil, add the peanuts, making sure they're submerged. Fry for 12 to 15 minutes, until light to medium brown. Use the strainer or spider to transfer them to the paper towel–lined mixing bowl. Shake gently to remove excess oil. Remove and discard the paper towel from the bowl. Add the fried shallots and garlic to the peanuts, season with salt, and toss together. Taste and adjust the salt as needed before serving.

Store leftovers in an airtight jar at room temperature for up to 3 weeks in the pantry.

Adobo Fries

Following the same formula as Canadian poutine or loaded fries, this recipe calls for coating crispy French fries in a sweet and sticky adobo sauce. The key to keeping the fries as crisp as can be, even after saucing them, is making sure the adobo sauce has fully thickened. Opting for a bag of frozen french fries makes this recipe super simple.

SERVES 4

½ cup (120 ml) water, plus a splash

1 tablespoon cornstarch

½ cup (120 ml) soy sauce

¼ cup (60 g) packed dark brown sugar

2 tablespoons cane vinegar

6 dried bay leaves

2 large garlic cloves, peeled and grated

Freshly cracked black pepper

4 cups (1 L) neutral oil such as vegetable, grapeseed, or avocado, for frying

1 package (32 ounces/900 g) frozen french fries

1 scallion, trimmed and chopped

Combine a splash of water with the cornstarch in a small bowl and stir until smooth. Set aside.

Combine the soy sauce, water, brown sugar, vinegar, bay leaves, and garlic in a saucepan and place it over medium-low heat. Bring to a gentle simmer and cook for 7 to 8 minutes, until reduced. Slowly add the cornstarch slurry, stirring vigorously to avoid clumps. Reduce the heat and continue to simmer for another 3 to 4 minutes, until no raw cornstarch flavor remains and the sauce is smooth, stirring occasionally to prevent the mixture from thickening too much. Add a few turns of freshly cracked black pepper and stir to combine. Remove from heat, remove and discard the bay leaves, and set aside.

Heat the oil in a large heavy-bottomed pot, such as a Dutch oven or cast-iron saucepan, over medium-high heat until it reaches 375°F (190°C). Line a large mixing bowl with paper towels.

(continued)

Drop a single fry into the oil to test if the oil is hot enough for frying. Once the oil bubbles around it, remove the tester fry using a slotted spoon or mesh spider. Carefully drop a handful of fries into the pot. Fry each batch for 10 to 12 minutes, until golden brown. Use the spoon or spider to transfer the cooked fries to the paper towel–lined mixing bowl and shake gently to remove any excess oil.

When the last batch of fries is almost finished, reheat the sauce over medium heat for 2 minutes. Once all the fries are cooked and drained, remove the paper towels and slightly tilt the bowl so all the fries are on one side. Pour ¼ cup (60 ml) of the adobo sauce into the other side of the bowl, then toss the fries with the sauce by slightly shaking the bowl in a circular motion and lightly lifting the fries over and over again. Taste the fries and add more sauce if needed, making sure each fry is evenly coated but not drenched. Garnish with the scallions and serve immediately.

Store any leftover adobo sauce in an airtight container for up to a week in the refrigerator.

Steamed Mushroom Buns

SIOPAO MUSHROOM ASADO

Steamed buns were introduced to the Philippines by Chinese immigrants in the 1920s and quickly became a go-to afternoon snack. These pillow-like buns are filled with a savory mushroom mix and gently steamed until soft and fluffy. Make a batch ahead of time to store in your freezer and reheat for a convenient and delicious snack.

MAKES 12 TO 15 MINI BUNS

BUNS

- ¾ cup plus 1 tablespoon (180 ml) lukewarm (about 100°F/38°C) water
- 1 tablespoon granulated sugar
- 1 teaspoon instant yeast
- 2 cups (250 g) all-purpose flour, plus more for the work surface
- Pinch of kosher salt
- 1 tablespoon vegetable oil

FILLING

- 1 shallot or 1 medium onion, peeled
- 3 garlic cloves, peeled
- 12 ounces (340 g) oyster mushrooms
- 1 tablespoon neutral oil such as vegetable, grapeseed, or avocado
- ¼ cup (60 ml) hoisin sauce, plus more for serving
- ¼ cup (60 ml) soy sauce
- 1 tablespoon brown sugar
- Pinch of kosher salt
- ¼ teaspoon black pepper
- 2 tablespoons water
- 1 tablespoon cornstarch

Combine the warm water, granulated sugar, and yeast in a measuring cup and stir until the yeast has dissolved.

Place the flour and salt in a large mixing bowl and stir together using a spatula. Make a well in the center. Slowly pour the water-yeast mixture into the well. Add the oil and gently mix everything together using a fork, incorporating the flour slowly into the well from the outside in. Once the dough is shaggy, press it together until it forms into a loose ball in the bowl.

(continued)

Transfer the dough to a lightly floured work surface and knead by folding the dough onto itself and pressing it down with the palm of your dominant hand. Do this for about 10 minutes, until the dough is smooth and supple.

Roll the dough into a ball and return it to the mixing bowl. Cover it with a clean kitchen towel and let it rest for 1 hour or until it has doubled in size.

While the dough is resting, make the filling. Finely chop the shallot and mince the garlic. Gently break the mushrooms apart into large, flat pieces. Brush the dirt off them with a pastry brush. Chop the mushrooms into ½- to 1-inch (1 to 2 cm) pieces and set them aside.

Pour the oil into a heavy-bottomed skillet and add the shallot and garlic. Place over medium-high heat and cook for 2 to 3 minutes, until softened. Add the mushrooms and stir to combine. Cook for 5 to 6 minutes, until the water in the mushrooms has been released and the edges start to brown.

Add the hoisin sauce, soy sauce, brown sugar, salt, and pepper and cook for 2 to 3 minutes, until sugars have dissolved. Combine the water and cornstarch in a small bowl and stir together until smooth. Reduce the heat, then slowly add the cornstarch slurry and stir vigorously to prevent clumps. Stir in a splash of water if the filling seems too thick, making sure it still has that sticky consistency. Remove from heat and let cool for about 15 minutes.

Once the dough has doubled in size, scoop it out of the bowl with a spatula and place it on the lightly floured work surface. Knead the dough for about 5 minutes to expel excess gas.

Shape the dough into a ball, then lightly flatten it into a rectangle. Using a knife or bench scraper, cut the dough halfway through down the center. Grab the two narrow ends and gently stretch and roll into a log 12 to 15 inches (30 to 40 cm) long. Use a sharp knife to divide the dough into 12 equal pieces. Cover them with a towel to rest for another 10 minutes.

Working with one piece of dough at a time and keeping the others covered, flatten the dough into a disk using a rolling pin on the lightly floured work surface. Rotate the disk and use the rolling pin to thin out the edges, keeping the center thick. Do this until you have a 4-inch (10 cm) round. Set aside and repeat with the rest of the pieces of dough.

Place a dough round in the palm of your nondominant hand and add a heaping tablespoon of the filling right in the center. Lightly flatten the filling to make sure it's even. Seal the bun by pulling the dough up over the filling and pinching the edge together with your dominant thumb and index finger to create a pleat. Continue to pull, pinch, and pleat the edge while twisting the bun until all the pleats meet the center. Firmly press the top together to seal the bun. Set the bun aside and repeat until you have 12 sealed buns.

Bring 2 to 3 inches (5 to 8 cm) water to a boil in a large pot. Line a bamboo steamer with parchment paper. Working in batches, add a few buns to the steamer, making sure to not overcrowd the steamer, to prevent the buns from sticking together. Place the cover on the steamer, place the steamer in the pot, and let the buns steam for 20 minutes or until fluffy and slightly glossy.

Remove the lid from the steamer using tongs and carefully remove the steamer from the pot. Gently take the buns off the parchment paper and set them aside to keep warm as you cook the rest of the buns. Replenish the water if it gets too low. Steam the remaining buns.

Serve the buns hot, with extra hoisin sauce on the side.

Store leftovers in a heavy resealable bag in the freezer for up to 2 months. Reheat from frozen by steaming them for 15 to 20 minutes.

Chickpea Spring Rolls

LUMPIANG GARBANZO

Chickpeas are by no means a traditional lumpia filling, but this recipe proves that you don't need fresh vegetables to make tasty spring rolls. The combination of hoisin sauce and onions makes for a sweet and salty flavor you won't find in any other lumpia recipe. These are best paired with a dipping sauce like sawsawan (page 48) for a touch of acidity to balance the hearty chickpea filling.

MAKES 12 TO 15 LUMPIA

1 medium white onion, peeled

4 ounces (110 g) green beans

Kosher salt and black pepper

1 cup (185 g) canned chickpeas, rinsed and drained

2 tablespoons hoisin sauce

1 package (16 ounces/454 g) 8 × 8-inch (20 × 20 cm) spring roll wrappers, thawed if frozen

2 cups (480 ml) neutral oil such as vegetable, grapeseed, or avocado, for frying

Daily Dipping Sauce (page 48), for serving

Slice the onion in half vertically, then slice each half into thin half-moons. Align the bottom ends of the green beans on a cutting board and trim off the stem ends. Slice the beans crosswise in half. Combine the onions and green beans in a bowl and season with a pinch of salt. Using your hands, toss to make sure they're well seasoned.

Combine the chickpeas with hoisin sauce, a pinch of salt, and about ¼ teaspoon of pepper in a separate mixing bowl. Mix thoroughly until the chickpeas are evenly coated.

To assemble the lumpia, follow the guide on page 117. Add 2 to 3 green bean pieces, a couple of onion slices, and 1 tablespoon of the chickpeas for each lumpia. (If you have any wrappers left, wrap the package well in plastic or put it in a heavy resealable bag or airtight container, and put them back in the freezer for another time.)

Once you've rolled all the lumpia, transfer them to a heavy resealable plastic bag or airtight container and freeze for about 1 hour to firm them up.

When you're ready to cook, remove as many lumpia from the freezer as you need and fry them immediately. (Keep any extras in the freezer for up to a month until you need them. Thaw frozen lumpia at room temperature for 30 minutes before frying.)

Fit a wire rack inside a rimmed baking sheet. Heat the oil in a large heavy-bottomed skillet over medium-high heat. Drop in a small piece of a wrapper to make sure the oil is hot enough for frying; the oil will bubble around it once it's ready. Alternatively, you can use a wooden chopstick to check; bubbles should form around the end when it is inserted in the oil.

Gently place 5 or 6 lumpia (or as many as you can fit) seam side down in the skillet, making sure they don't stick to each other. Fry on one side for 2 to 3 minutes, until golden brown, then flip and fry the other side until golden. Reduce the heat to medium-low if the lumpia seem to be browning too quickly. Transfer the cooked lumpia with tongs to the wire rack to drain. Continue to fry in batches. Serve the lumpia hot with the dipping sauce.

Vermicelli Spring Rolls

LUMPIANG VERMICELLI

This recipe takes inspiration from the Vietnamese spring rolls (chả giò) wrapped in rice paper and deep-fried. Using seasoned vermicelli noodles, this recipe is prepared the same way as the other traditional fried lumpia, but instead of being deep-fried, they're shallow-fried until golden brown and served with banana ketchup for an extra touch of Filipino flair.

MAKES 12 TO 15 LUMPIA

- 4 garlic cloves, peeled
- 1 large carrot, peeled
- 12 ounces (340 g) king oyster mushrooms, cleaned (see page 98)
- 2 cups (180 g) bean sprouts
- Kosher salt and black pepper
- 7 ounces (200 g) rice vermicelli noodles
- 1 tablespoon granulated sugar
- 1 tablespoon soy sauce
- 1 package (16 ounces/454 g) 8 × 8-inch (20 × 20 cm) spring roll wrappers, thawed if frozen
- 2 cups (480 ml) neutral oil such as vegetable, grapeseed, or avocado, for frying
- Banana ketchup, for serving

Mince the garlic and transfer to a large mixing bowl. Shred the carrots into the same bowl on the large holes of a box grater.

Working one at a time, place a mushroom on the cutting board. Holding the cap down with one fork, use another fork to carefully tug the flesh with a downward pulling motion, alternating sides. Add the shredded mushrooms to the carrots and garlic. Add the bean sprouts. Season with a pinch of salt and pepper and toss together using your hands to combine.

Bring a large pot of water to a boil over high heat. Add the vermicelli noodles, pushing them down with tongs to make sure they are submerged. Check the package instructions for the cook time—most brands take about 2 minutes. Stir the noodles to prevent them from sticking. Once the noodles are cooked, drain them in a fine-mesh strainer and rinse with cold water. Drain well.

Transfer the cooked noodles to a separate large mixing bowl. Add the sugar, soy sauce, and a large pinch each of salt and pepper, and stir to combine. Using kitchen shears, cut the noodles into short pieces to make them easier to work with.

To assemble the lumpia, follow the guide on page 117. Use 2 tablespoons of the vegetable mixture and 2 tablespoons of the noodles on top. (If you have any wrappers left, wrap the package well in plastic or put it in a heavy resealable bag or airtight container, and put them back in the freezer for another time.)

Once you've rolled all of the lumpia, transfer them to a heavy resealable bag or airtight container and freeze for about 1 hour to firm them up.

When you're ready to cook, remove as many lumpia from the freezer as you need and fry them immediately. (Keep any extras in the freezer for up to a month until you need them. Thaw frozen lumpia at room temperature for 30 minutes before frying.)

Fit a wire rack inside a rimmed baking sheet. Heat the oil in a large heavy-bottomed skillet over medium-high heat. Drop in a small piece of a wrapper to make sure the oil is hot enough for frying; the oil will bubble around it once it's ready. Alternatively, you can use a wooden chopstick to check; bubbles should form around the end when it is inserted in the oil.

Gently place 5 or 6 lumpia (or as many as you can fit) seam side down in the skillet, making sure they don't stick to each other. Fry on one side for 2 to 3 minutes, until golden brown, then flip and fry the other side until golden. Reduce the heat to medium-low if the lumpia seem to be browning too quickly. Transfer the cooked lumpia with tongs to the wire rack to drain. Continue to fry in batches. Serve the lumpia hot with banana ketchup for dipping.

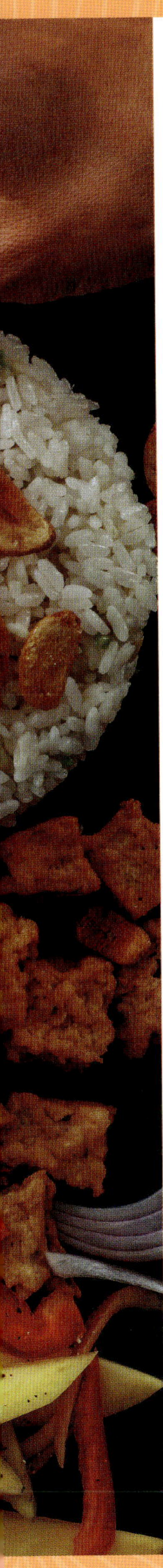

The Kamayan Way

Kamayan is a traditional act of eating with your hands without using any plates or utensils. Various dishes, from fried finger foods like lumpia to sweet and saucy stews like adobo, are laid out on a spread of banana leaves. While the practice of using your bare hands to eat has been around since the beginning of time, laying out food on banana leaves came from Filipino soldiers gathering to eat quickly. The cleanup proved to be as easy as rolling up the leaves and throwing them in the compost all at once without worrying about washing plates or utensils. Today, the kamayan practice is used in communal feasts and has even traveled to Filipino restaurants found in the West. The tactile nature of eating with your hands keeps you in tune with the communal activity that is sharing a meal with the people you love. The experience is as joyful as it is intimate—and, of course, delicious.

PREPARATION

Setting up for a kamayan feast is easier than you might think, and it doesn't have to be just for a large group, either. Depending on how many people you're hosting, you'll need to ensure you have enough banana leaves to present the food. If fresh banana leaves are difficult to access, you can buy them frozen from Asian or Latin supermarkets and thaw them for at least half an hour before setting up your table.

For a crowd, you'll want to cover the entire dining table with banana leaves. For a smaller group of three or four people, arrange banana leaves on a rimmed baking sheet and use that to serve. For the food to offer, a good rule of thumb is to serve rice with one protein, one vegetable dish (such as Vegetable Spring Rolls, page 115), one fruit dish, and a couple of dipping sauces. From there, you can make tweaks and add more of what you want.

The key to laying out the food is balance. Make sure to spread out the food evenly. If you have rice in one corner, the opposite corner and the middle should get some, too. This prevents people from constantly bumping elbows and reaching over each other at the table. Remember to leave space around the food to give your guests some room for drinks or to place their food down.

MENU IDEAS

For a large crowd of six to ten people, this assortment of dishes will complete a full kamayan menu:

Vegetable Spring Rolls (115)

Roasted Mushrooms with Sticky Adobo Sauce (95)

Stir-Fried Squash with Okra, Long Beans, and Eggplant (82)

Crispy Pan-Fried Tofu (46)

Quick Pan-Fried Eggplant in Soy Sauce (41)

Garlic Fried Rice (21)

Vegetable Stir-Fried Noodles (109)

Tangy Pickled Papaya (43)

Also offer sliced mangoes, sliced pineapple, and a selection of dipping sauces.

For a group of three to six people, try this mix:

Spicy Curried Taro Leaves (85)

Sizzling Mushroom and Tofu Sisig (101)

Filipino-Style Tofu Sausage (25)

Green Mango Salad (35)

Add grilled corn on the cob, sliced cucumbers, steamed jasmine rice, and a selection of dipping sauces.

The concept of kamayan doesn't have to end at large Filipino gatherings. In fact, you can take this approach to your grazing tables. Next time you host a group of friends, you can lay out a few long sheets of parchment paper to cover your dining table and place your snacks right on top, the same way you would if you were to use a board. That way, when it comes to cleaning up, you can easily roll up the parchment paper and throw it away or compost it.

HOW TO EAT WITH YOUR HANDS

Eating with your hands might seem as simple as picking up food and popping it in your mouth. But there is a technique: Scoop up a pinch or piece of food using your dominant hand. Use your thumb to push it into your mouth. Keep your nondominant clean for passing things to other guests or drinking.

When you'll be eating with your hands, make sure to ask your guests to wash their hands before the meal. This should be a given, but it doesn't hurt to remind people. You could also use food-safe disposable gloves for ease.

Sweets & Treats

Filipino desserts and delicacies are often whimsical adaptions of dishes you already know and love. Ice cream flavored with ube, cakes baked with cassava, and drinks made with pineapple or calamansi are just some of the rainbow of choices.

Banana Fritters, Two Ways

MARUYA

With all due respect to banana bread, these fritters are the more convenient solution for your overripe banana dilemma. With only 30 minutes and less cleanup, you can make these crispy-on-the-outside, fluffy-on-the-inside fritters. Traditionally, maruya are made with Saba bananas, a short and thick cultivar of banana originating in the Philippines, but you can easily use regular bananas as a substitute.

There are two ways to make maruya, depending on the ripeness of your bananas. The mashed method is ideal for overripe bananas that have lost their structural integrity, while the fan method is preferable for bananas that are perfectly ripe. Both methods result in a crispy outer layer and a sweet, velvety interior. No matter your expertise on frying foods, this batter is so forgiving, it's impossible to mess it up.

SERVES 2 OR 3

½ cup (100 g) granulated sugar
⅓ cup (42 g) all-purpose flour
1 tablespoon cornstarch
1 tablespoon dark brown sugar
1 teaspoon baking powder
1 teaspoon pure vanilla extract
Pinch of kosher salt
¼ cup (60 ml) water
2 large bananas or 4 Saba bananas, peeled
¼ cup (60 ml) neutral oil such as vegetable, grapeseed, or avocado, for frying

Pour the granulated sugar into a shallow bowl or rimmed dinner plate. Line a rimmed baking sheet with paper towels and fit a wire rack inside.

Combine the flour, cornstarch, brown sugar, baking powder, vanilla, salt, and water in a large mixing bowl. Whisk together until it looks like pancake batter, making sure not to overmix. Lumps are okay.

(continued)

Mashed Method

Mash the bananas in a separate bowl, making sure to still leave some large pieces. Add to the batter and mix everything with a spatula until well combined.

Fan Method

If using large bananas, cut them in half crosswise first. Slice the bananas in half lengthwise and place them on the cutting board with the flat side down. Working with one at a time, carefully slice the bananas lengthwise into thirds, leaving about ½ inch (1 cm) connected at the bottom. Gently spread out the pieces like a fan and set them aside on a baking sheet or large dinner plate.

Heat a large heavy-bottomed or cast-iron skillet over medium heat for about 3 minutes. Add the oil, and let it heat up for another minute.

Working in batches, scoop 2 tablespoons of mashed batter into the pan for each fritter and lightly flatten so they will cook evenly, making sure they don't stick to each other. Or working with one banana fan at a time, dip it in the batter to fully coat it, then place it in the oil; do only as many fans as will fit in the pan without sticking to each other.

Fry the fritters for 3 to 5 minutes, until medium to golden brown on the bottom, then flip and fry the other side until brown, another 3 to 5 minutes. Gently remove the cooked fritters from the oil with a slotted spatula and transfer them to the wire rack to drain. Repeat until the batter and bananas are used up.

While they're still hot but cool enough to touch, roll fritters one at a time in the granulated sugar, making sure both sides are coated. Serve immediately while still hot.

Banana Chips

Reminiscent of the ones you'd find in Filipino food stalls, these banana chips are fried twice and coated with syrup, making them delightfully crispy and sweet. This recipe requires adding syrup to the oil, so wear your oven mitts and proceed with caution! Serve them as part of a snack table or grazing board, or as a sweet appetizer—they'll be gone before you know it.

SERVES 4 TO 6

5 large unripe Saba bananas or 2 unripe green plantains (about 1.2 pounds/550 g total)

½ cup (100 g) granulated sugar

½ cup (120 ml) boiling water

¼ teaspoon kosher salt

3 cups (720 ml) neutral oil such as vegetable, grapeseed, or avocado, for frying

Carefully peel the bananas using a paring knife. Slice them into paper-thin rounds using the narrowest setting of a mandoline. If you don't own a mandoline, use a chef's knife to cut the banana into thin slices, making sure to take your time and work carefully.

Combine the sugar, boiling water, and salt in a small bowl and stir together until the sugar dissolves. Set aside to cool.

Fit a wire rack inside a rimmed baking sheet.

Pour the oil into a wok or heavy-bottomed skillet and place it over medium-low heat. Make sure to wear oven mitts to avoid the oil splashing onto your skin. Once the oil reaches about 375°F (190°C) on a deep-fry thermometer, gently drop the banana slices into the oil, working in batches and carefully placing them in one at a time to prevent them from sticking together. Fry for 3 to 5 minutes, just until lightly golden. Gently transfer the banana chips to the wire rack using a fine-mesh strainer, slotted spoon, or mesh spider. Continue to fry in batches until all of them have been cooked.

Reduce the heat to low and let the oil cool to 330°F (165°C). Transfer all the banana chips back into the oil. Working with caution and using oven mitts to protect your arms from hot oil, add 5 tablespoons (75 ml) of the

(continued)

syrup and gently stir the chips to make sure the syrup sticks. The syrup will coat the chips and add a crunchy exterior. Take a step back to avoid the oil splashing onto your skin. Continue to stir for another 2 to 3 minutes or until the chips are just golden and shiny. You'll want to keep an eye out and make sure the chips don't get too dark. Remove them using the strainer or slotted spoon and spread them out evenly on the wire rack to drain any excess oil and prevent them from sticking together.

Let the chips cool for 10 minutes before serving, or transfer them into an airtight container and store them at room temperature for up to 2 weeks.

Steamed Rice Cakes Wrapped in Banana Leaves

SUMAN

Suman is one of the many types of rice cake wrapped in banana leaves and steamed until it turns sticky and chewy. Using a bamboo steamer, the steam from the hot water rises and gently cooks the suman evenly, transforming it into a fluffy cake that lands somewhere in between rice pudding and mochi. This rice cake is usually served for breakfast or as an afternoon snack, and is best paired with coconut jam for sweetness and cold sliced mangoes for freshness.

SERVES 6 TO 8

SUMAN

2 cups (380 g) glutinous rice

1 package (16 ounces/454 g) frozen banana leaves

1 can (400 ml) coconut milk

½ cup (120 ml) water

½ cup (110 g) packed dark brown sugar

¼ teaspoon kosher salt

COCO JAM

1 can (400 g) coconut cream

1 cup (185 g) muscovado sugar or dark brown sugar

⅛ teaspoon kosher salt

2 tablespoons Golden Coconut Curd (page 51), for garnish

Rinse the rice two or three times in a fine-mesh strainer under cold water until the water runs clear. Set aside to drain.

Cut the banana leaves into 9 × 5-inch (22 × 13 cm) rectangles with the longer side following the leaf veins. Set aside 12 to 14 pieces.

Combine the coconut milk, water, brown sugar, and salt in a large heavy-bottomed pot and place over medium heat. Bring to a simmer. Add the

(continued)

rice and stir to combine. Reduce the heat to medium-low and simmer for 10 minutes or until slightly thickened.

Remove from heat and cool for 5 minutes. (You're not cooking the rice all the way through at this point, but it should have absorbed most of the liquid.)

Lay out a banana leaf rectangle on a clean work surface with the longer side facing you. Place 3 to 4 tablespoons of the rice mixture in the center of the banana leaf. Form the rice into a log. Bring up the bottom edge of the leaf to cover the rice, fold in the left and right sides, then roll it up from the bottom. The rice should be sticky enough to hold the packet together. Repeat until you have filled all the banana leaves.

Line a bamboo steamer or metal steamer basket with parchment paper. Place 2 or 3 packets (or as many as you can fit without overcrowding) in the steamer. Bring 2 to 3 inches (5 to 8 cm) water to a boil in a large, deep pot. Carefully place the steamer in the pot, cover, and steam the packets for 40 minutes. (Periodically check the water level and add more boiling water if it's low.) Repeat until all the packets have been steamed.

In the meantime, combine the coconut cream, muscovado sugar, and salt in a medium saucepan and place it over medium heat. Stir until the sugar dissolves. Reduce the heat to medium-low and simmer for 40 minutes, occasionally scraping the sides of the pan. Once the mixture turns a toffee-like color and consistency, remove it from the heat and let it cool for at least 10 minutes. Set aside until you're ready to serve.

Remove the suman from the steamer using tongs and let cool for 5 to 10 minutes on a large dinner plate. If serving immediately, open each packet and carefully remove the cooked suman. Pile them on a serving platter with a heavy drizzle of coco jam and a sprinkle of coconut curd, and serve.

Store any leftovers with the banana leaf wrappers intact in the refrigerator for up to 4 days. Transfer any leftover coco jam to a sterilized jar and store in the refrigerator for up to 2 weeks. Reheat in the microwave for about 30 seconds before serving.

Sweet and Sticky Coconut Rice Cake

BIKO

Biko is a fragrant, chewy rice cake, similar to sticky toffee pudding, served with a coconut caramel topping. The rice is cooked twice: first simmered in a pot of coconut cream to develop a nutty depth of flavor, then baked with syrup to enhance its sweetness. This traditional recipe is often served for breakfast, dessert, or a midafternoon snack.

SERVES 6 TO 8

COCONUT SYRUP

1 can (400 ml) coconut cream

1 cup (220 g) packed dark brown sugar

⅛ teaspoon kosher salt

1 tablespoon coconut oil, melted

RICE

2 cups (380 g) glutinous rice, rinsed and drained well

1 can (400 ml) coconut milk

¼ teaspoon kosher salt

Pinch of flaky sea salt (optional)

1 tablespoon Golden Coconut Curd (page 51; optional)

Pour the coconut cream into a saucepan and cook over medium heat for 5 minutes or until slightly reduced. Add the brown sugar and salt and stir to combine. Simmer for another 30 to 35 minutes, stirring occasionally to prevent the sugar from burning. The coconut syrup should be deep golden brown. Remove from heat and set aside to cool.

Preheat the oven to 350°F (175°C). Grease an 8 × 8-inch (20 × 20 cm) cake pan with the coconut oil.

Combine the rice and coconut milk in a large heavy-bottomed pot. Add the kosher salt and stir to combine. Cook over medium heat for 15 minutes or until tender all the way through, stirring occasionally to prevent the rice from sticking.

(continued)

Add half of the syrup to the rice. Mix together until the syrup is evenly distributed. Transfer the rice to the greased cake pan and flatten it out evenly using an offset spatula. Pour the remainder of the syrup over top, spreading it with the back of a spoon to make sure the rice is evenly covered.

Bake for 25 minutes or until the syrup on top has thickened and created a sticky toffee–like layer. Let the rice cake cool for 15 minutes before sprinkling flaky sea salt or golden coconut curd on top, if you like. Cool for another 10 minutes before slicing into squares.

Store any leftovers in an airtight container in the refrigerator for up to 3 days. Reheat in the microwave for 30 seconds before serving.

The Versatility of Coconuts

Though the exact origin of this tropical fruit is still unknown (some believe it's from Southeast Asia; others think it's from South America), coconut was always an essential part of Filipino cuisine—and culture—long before it became popular in the West. In fact, the Philippines is widely known as one of the top coconut producers in the world.

The tree produces a honey-like sap used to make tuba (wine), sukang tuba (vinegar), and unrefined coconut sugar. The wine is sometimes used as an offering in traditional rituals; the vinegar is a popular condiment used to brighten up dishes or as a dipping sauce for salty foods; you can use the sugar as an alternative to brown sugar.

The sweet and refreshing juice you release by opening the fruit is just as versatile. It's often served at resorts and beach restaurants; you can purchase it in cans or Tetrapaks from grocery and convenience stores and use it as a base for smoothies and mocktails.

The crown jewel of the coconut is the flesh, which Filipinos use in sweet and savory applications. In its fresh and raw form, coconut meat is slightly sweet and nutty. It's often shredded and used as a sweet filling in desserts such as cakes and pies. Once cooked, it softens to a jelly-like texture, which naturally adds chewiness without pectin. Coconut milk, made by pureeing the flesh with water, then squeezing out the rich liquid, is a naturally high-fat ingredient, providing an aroma, nutty flavor, and velvety texture that cannot be replaced by other plant-based milks. Coconut milk and cream, the fatty liquid that rises to the top (just like dairy cream), add richness to stews and curries like Spicy Curried Taro Leaves (page 85) and to some traditional desserts, such as Cassava Cake (page 170).

In true Filipino fashion, no part of the coconut goes to waste, not even those furry brown coconut husks. Farmers break the husks down to manufacture other products like brushes, which are made by attaching the fibers to a wooden handle. The fibers are also utilized to produce other items like twine, doormats, plant holders, and fertilizer, making the coconut an abundant source of eco-friendly tools. Coconuts, from inside out, are deeply ingrained in the Filipino way of life and a valuable staple in its cuisine.

Flat Rice Cakes in Coconut Syrup

PALITAW SA LATIK

Rice cakes are small, soft and chewy disks, widely eaten across Southeast Asia in both savory and sweet applications. They're much easier to make than most baked desserts—all you have to do is mix the dough, shape the cakes, and boil! Finished with a coating of sweet and nutty coconut syrup, they're irresistible. Serve these sweet rice cakes for breakfast, dessert, or as a midafternoon snack, paired with your favorite hot drink.

SERVES 6 TO 10

RICE CAKES

2 cups (240 g) glutinous rice flour

1 cup (240 ml) coconut milk

¼ teaspoon kosher salt

COCONUT SYRUP

1 can (400 ml) coconut cream

1 cup (220 g) packed dark brown sugar

⅛ teaspoon kosher salt

2 tablespoons Golden Coconut Curd (page 51), for garnish (optional)

Combine the glutinous rice flour, coconut milk, and salt in a large mixing bowl. Mix with a wooden spoon or spatula for 3 to 4 minutes, until a smooth dough forms.

To form the rice cakes, scoop up 2 tablespoons of the dough and roll it into a ball using the palms of your hands. Gently flatten the ball into a ½- to 1-inch-thick (1 to 2 cm) patty and set it aside on a baking sheet. Repeat with the remaining dough until you have used it up.

Combine the coconut cream, brown sugar, and salt in a large saucepan. Place over medium heat, bring to a boil, and cook for 15 minutes, stirring occasionally, until slightly reduced. Remove from heat and set aside to keep warm.

Bring a pot of water to a boil. Gently add the rice cakes to the boiling water, working with 3 or 4 rice cakes at a time to prevent them from sticking to each other. Cook for 3 minutes or until they float to the surface. Scoop the cooked rice cakes out using a fine-mesh sieve or mesh spider, drain briefly, and add them to the warm coconut syrup.

Serve the rice cakes immediately with a little of the syrup, sprinkled with golden coconut curd if you like.

Glutinous Rice Balls in Coconut Soup

GINATAANG BILO BILO

This sweet and creamy dessert soup boasts a medley of textures in every bite. It's assembled from chewy rice balls made with ube extract for an earthy, vanilla-like flavor and gorgeous purple color, accompanied by bananas, jackfruit, and sago pearls, all submerged in a sweet and warm coconut soup. It's best served hot and can also be eaten for breakfast.

SERVES 4 TO 6

BILO BILO

1 cup (120 g) glutinous rice flour

½ cup (120 ml) water

2 teaspoons ube extract

SOUP

3 Saba bananas or 2 ripe plantains, peeled

1 can (20 ounces/565 g) jackfruit in syrup, drained

½ cup (70 g) sago pearls

1 can (400 ml) coconut milk

1 cup (240 ml) water

⅓ cup (65 g) granulated sugar, plus more as needed

Combine the glutinous rice flour, water, and ube extract in a large mixing bowl and stir together using a spatula until it forms a smooth dough. Scoop up about 1 tablespoon of the dough, roll it into a ball between the palms of your hands, and set aside on a large plate. Repeat until you've used up all the dough. You should have about 18 to 20 balls.

Slice the bananas into ½-inch-thick (1 cm) rounds and set aside on a plate. Slice the jackfruit into ½-inch (1 cm) strips and set aside with the bananas.

Bring a pot of water to a boil over medium-high heat. Add the sago pearls and stir. Cook for 15 minutes or until the pearls are completely translucent. Drain the pearls in a fine-mesh strainer, rinse in cold water for 30 seconds, and set aside.

Combine the coconut milk, water, and sugar in a medium heavy-bottomed saucepan and place over medium-high heat. Bring to a boil, stirring occasionally. Once vigorously boiling, reduce the heat to medium.

Add the bananas and cook for 2 to 3 minutes, until slightly soft. Add the rice balls one at a time and stir to combine. Cook for 3 to 5 minutes, until the rice balls start to float and the bananas are tender. Add the jackfruit and stir again. At this point, you can add a bit more water to adjust the consistency. Taste the soup and adjust the sweetness. Add the sago pearls and give everything a good mix. Simmer the soup for another 2 to 3 minutes to bring all the flavors together, then remove from heat. Serve the bilo bilo immediately in heat-proof dessert bowls.

Store leftovers in an airtight container for up to a week. Reheat in the microwave for 1 to 2 minutes.

Creamy Strawberry and Mango Sago

MANGGA SAGO

This cold dessert soup is a twist on Hong Kong's mango pomelo sago. Combining the fresh mango with strawberries and chewy sago pearls makes this a fun and refreshing dessert you'll want to have every day of the summer. Use either ripe Carabao or Ataúlfo mangoes for best results.

SERVES 4 TO 6

2 ripe yellow mangoes, such as Carabao or Ataúlfo, cold

1 cup (150 g) fresh strawberries, cold

1 can (200 ml) coconut milk

⅓ cup (80 ml) sweetened condensed plant-based milk, plus more as needed

¼ teaspoon kosher salt

1 cup (150 g) dried sago or mini tapioca pearls

Cut off the mango cheeks by standing each mango on end and slicing straight down along the seed. Lay each cheek skin side down on a cutting board and carefully scoop the fruit out using a large spoon, making sure to keep the whole cheek intact. Place the flat side down on the cutting board and cube the mango cheek into bite-sized chunks. Set aside half of the mango cubes in a bowl; transfer the rest to a blender.

Remove the leafy tops and cores of the strawberries. Slice the strawberries into ¼-inch-thick (6 mm) pieces. Set aside half of the strawberries in another bowl; transfer the rest to the blender along with the mango cubes.

Add the coconut milk, condensed milk, and salt to the blender and blend until smooth. Transfer the puree to a large airtight container. Chill in the freezer for about 20 minutes or in the refrigerator for 1 hour.

Bring a pot of water to a boil over medium-high heat. Add the sago pearls and stir. Cook for 15 minutes or until the pearls are completely translucent. Drain the pearls in a fine-mesh strainer, and rinse them in cold water until cold.

Remove the puree from the freezer or refrigerator and stir in the sago pearls. Serve in individual cups, topped with remainder of the mango chunks and strawberry slices.

Store any leftovers in the refrigerator for up to 3 days.

NOTE: *If sweetened condensed plant-based milk is too difficult to find, combine ⅓ cup (65 g) granulated sugar with 2 tablespoons water in a ramekin and microwave for 20 to 30 seconds, until the sugar is completely dissolved. Add this syrup plus an extra ¼ cup (60 ml) coconut milk to the mixture in the blender to keep the creaminess.*

No-Churn Ube Ice Cream

Ube is a beloved Filipino ingredient that has become a cultural symbol celebrated in desserts. Its taste is similar to sweet potato, but it boasts a tropical fragrance more akin to coconut and has a deep violet color. This recipe uses ube in two ways: the vegetable itself and the extract. Both ingredients are key to the ice cream's velvety texture and iconic purple hue.

MAKES 1 QUART

½ large ube (about 5 ounces/ 140 g), or ¼ cup (100 g) ube jam

2 cups (480 ml) plant-based heavy whipping cream such as Silk or Califia, chilled

1 can (11.25 ounces/320 g) sweetened condensed plant-based milk

4 teaspoons (20 ml) ube extract

1 teaspoon pure vanilla extract

If using fresh ubes, peel the skin, cut them into quarters, and cook them in a pot of boiling water until tender, about 10 to 15 minutes. Remove from heat and drain off the water. Mash the ube using a fork or potato masher until smooth. Set aside to cool completely. (If using ube jam, skip this step.)

Whisk the whipping cream in another mixing bowl using an electric hand mixer. Begin to whisk on low speed for 2 minutes. Increase the speed to medium and continue to whisk for 1 minute until it begins to thicken. Add the condensed milk and continue to whisk for 1 to 2 minutes, until combined.

Add the mashed ube or ube jam, ube extract, and vanilla, and whisk for 1 minute or until the mixture holds stiff peaks. Transfer the mixture to a freezer-safe container, cover tightly, and freeze for 4 to 6 hours or overnight. Serve 1 to 2 scoops of the chilled ice cream in a small bowl or cone. Keep in the freezer for up to 2 months.

NOTE: *If sweetened condensed plant-based milk is difficult to find, combine ½ cup (100 g) granulated sugar, a pinch of salt, and 3 tablespoons of water in a ramekin and microwave for 20 to 30 seconds, until the sugar is completely dissolved. Use this syrup plus an extra ⅓ cup (80 ml) heavy whipping cream to replace the condensed milk.*

Fried Twisted Doughnuts

BICHO-BICHO

Bicho-bicho is the perfect not-too-sweet dessert. These fluffy doughnuts are sold in most Filipino bakeries and by street vendors. A final dusting of granulated sugar coats each bite you take with a subtle crunch before you reach the fluffy interior. Serve the doughnuts warm along with a cup of freshly brewed coffee or tea.

MAKES 12 DOUGHNUTS

3¼ cups (405 g) all-purpose flour, plus more for the work surface

¼ cup (50 g) granulated sugar, plus ⅓ cup (66 g) for coating

2 teaspoons (6 g) instant yeast

½ teaspoon kosher salt

1 cup (240 ml) plant-based milk such as oat or almond, warmed to 110°F (43°C)

¼ cup (65 g) unsweetened applesauce

3 tablespoons plant-based butter, melted

Neutral oil such as vegetable, grapeseed, or avocado

2 teaspoons cinnamon powder (optional)

Add the flour, ¼ cup (50 g) sugar, the yeast, and salt to a large mixing bowl. Whisk together until combined, then make a well in the center. Pour the milk, applesauce, and butter into the well. Gently combine everything using a spatula by bringing a little bit of the flour mixture at a time from the outside into the center, making sure to scrape the sides of the bowl. Once the mixture turns into a shaggy dough, knead it in the bowl until you can form it into a cohesive ball.

Grease a clean large mixing bowl and your work surface with about 2 tablespoons oil. Transfer the dough to the work surface and continue to knead by folding the dough onto itself and using the palm of your hands to push it down. Repeat until the dough is smooth and elastic, about 5 to 7 minutes. Place the dough in the greased mixing bowl and cover it with a clean kitchen towel. Let the dough rest in a warm spot for 1 hour or until it has doubled in size.

Press down on the center of the dough to expel excess gas and relax the gluten. Lightly flour the work surface and turn out the dough onto it. Gently flatten the dough into a rectangle using your hands, making sure not to knead it again. (At this point, you don't want to overwork the dough because the doughnuts could end up being tough.)

Divide the dough into two even pieces, then roll them into 2 logs, about 6 to 7 inches (15 to 18 cm) long. Cut the dough into 12 pieces. Cover the dough with a clean kitchen towel while working with one at a time. Roll the piece into a 10- to 12-inch-long (25 to 30 cm) log. Create a "U" horseshoe shape, then gently fold it together in the center and tightly twist the two halves together, overlapping to create a twist. Press the ends of the dough firmly together to secure the knot, then gently press the rest of the braided dough to make sure it doesn't unravel. Place the shaped doughnut on a baking sheet. Repeat until you've twisted all of the doughnuts. Cover them with a clean kitchen towel to rest for another 15 to 20 minutes, until soft.

Place the sugar for coating and optional cinnamon powder in a large mixing bowl. Line a rimmed baking sheet with paper towels and fit a wire rack inside.

Add enough oil to a large heavy-bottomed pot to come 2 to 3 inches (5 to 8 cm) up the sides. Place the pot over medium-low heat. Once the oil is shimmering hot (about 350°F/175°C), fry the doughnuts in batches of 3 or 4, making sure they are not touching and the pot isn't overcrowded. Fry the doughnuts for 4 to 5 minutes on one side, until lightly golden, then flip using a mesh spider or slotted spoon and fry for another 4 to 5 minutes. Remove the doughnuts from the oil with the spider and place them on the wire rack to briefly drain any excess oil. While the doughnuts are still hot, add them to the bowl of sugar and gently toss to coat, making sure each side is evenly covered. Serve immediately while hot.

Store leftovers in an airtight container for up to 2 days at room temperature.

Sweet Banana Spring Rolls

TURON

This spring roll is filled with starchy banana and syrupy jackfruit, which become soft and caramelized, while the spring roll wrapper remains crunchy on the outside. You can't go wrong with having turon for dessert or an afternoon snack with a hot coffee or tea. Jackfruit is traditionally incorporated in turon, but if you can't find it, the banana will be a perfectly fine filling on its own.

MAKES 12 SPRING ROLLS

½ cup (110 g) packed dark brown sugar

6 Saba bananas or 3 ripe plantains, peeled

1 can (20 ounces/565 g) jackfruit in syrup, drained

Twelve 8 × 8-inch (20 × 20 cm) spring roll wrappers, thawed if frozen

¼ cup (60 ml) neutral oil such as vegetable, grapeseed, or avocado

Place the brown sugar on a plate and spread it out evenly. Slice the bananas lengthwise in half. If using plantains, first slice them in half horizontally, then slice each piece in half vertically. Roll the banana pieces in the sugar to coat. Reserve any leftover sugar.

Slice the jackfruit into ½- to 1-inch-thick (1 to 2 cm) sticks.

To assemble the lumpia, follow the guide on page 117. Place the flat side of the banana on the wrapper and add 2 or 3 pieces of jackfruit on top.

Fit a rimmed baking sheet with a wire rack. Heat the oil in a large heavy-bottomed skillet over medium heat. Drop in a small piece of a wrapper to make sure the oil is hot enough for frying; the oil will bubble around it once it's ready. Alternatively, you can use a wooden chopstick to check; bubbles should form around the end when it is inserted in the oil.

Add the reserved sugar to the oil and spread it out as much as you can with tongs or a silicone spatula. Be sure to wear oven mittens in case hot oil splatters. Working quickly, gently place 5 or 6 rolls (or as many as you can fit) in the skillet, making sure they don't stick to each other. Fry for 2 to 3 minutes, until the bottom is golden brown. Rotate each roll and fry until the bottom is golden. Keep rotating and frying until the rolls are golden brown all over. Transfer the cooked rolls to the wire rack to drain off excess oil. Fry the remainder of the rolls, in batches if necessary. Serve while hot.

Freestyle It

- Serve a couple of the Sweet Banana Spring Rolls with a scoop of **No-Churn Ube Ice Cream** (page 165) for a Filipino-style banana split.

Cassava Cake

Cassava, a nutty and starchy root vegetable, makes this cake plush and chewy, but the cake is still beginner-friendly. Coconut cream and sweetened condensed plant-based milk join forces to flavor the cake and the custard topping. This traditional Filipino cake is believed to have originated in Quezon during the Spanish colonial era, when cassava was first imported from Latin America. It is best served hot and goes well with any warm beverage. Look for cassava next to the potatoes in the grocery store or check the frozen vegetable section. Check the Resources (see page 183) for where to find the coconut strings (also called macapuno or coconut sport).

SERVES 4 TO 6

CAKE

4 tablespoons (60 g) plant-based butter or margarine, melted, plus more for greasing the pan

1 pound (450 g) shredded peeled cassava

1 can (400 ml) coconut milk

1 can (11.25 ounces/320 g) sweetened condensed plant-based milk

1 cup (300 g) jarred coconut strings, drained

½ cup (125 g) unsweetened applesauce

Pinch of kosher salt

CUSTARD TOPPING

¼ cup (60 ml) sweetened condensed plant-based milk

¼ cup (60 ml) coconut cream

1 tablespoon plant-based butter or margarine, softened

Pinch of kosher salt

Preheat the oven to 350°F (175°C). Grease an 8 × 8-inch (20 × 20 cm) cake pan with a little melted butter.

Combine the cassava, coconut milk, condensed milk, coconut strings, applesauce, melted butter, and salt in a large mixing bowl. Stir together to thoroughly combine. Pour the mixture into the greased pan and cover it with aluminum foil. Bake for 50 minutes or until firm.

Meanwhile, prepare the custard topping by combining the condensed milk, coconut cream, butter, and salt in a small saucepan over medium-low

(continued)

heat. Stir together and bring to a gentle simmer. Cook, stirring occasionally, until slightly thickened, about 5 to 8 minutes. The custard should be thick enough to coat the back of a spoon.

Pour the custard over the cake as soon as it comes out of the oven. (Do not turn the oven off.) Spread the custard evenly using an offset spatula. Place the cake back in the oven without the foil this time and bake for another 15 minutes, or until the top is caramelized.

Let the cake cool in the pan for about 1 hour at room temperature to firm up. Slice into squares and serve.

Cover leftovers with plastic wrap and store in the refrigerator for up to a week. Reheat in the microwave for 2 minutes.

NOTE: *If sweetened condensed plant-based milk is too difficult to find, combine ½ cup (100 g) granulated sugar with a pinch of salt and about 3 tablespoons of water in a ramekin and microwave for 20 to 30 seconds, until the sugar is completely dissolved. Use this syrup plus an extra ⅓ cup (80 ml) coconut cream to replace the condensed milk. Set aside ¼ cup (60 ml) for the topping and use the rest in the cake.*

Coconut Hand Pies

BUKO PIE

Jollibee, the Philippines' equivalent of McDonald's, is known for its savory fried foods and sweet spaghetti, but even better known for its luscious coconut hand pies. While making them from scratch isn't as simple as picking them up at the drive-thru, these buko pies are easier than most desserts thanks to store-bought puff pastry. To save even more time, you'll use store-bought coconut meat, too (check the Resources on page 183).

MAKES 6 HAND PIES

1 jar (12 ounces/340 g) coconut strings, drained

1 can (400 ml) coconut milk

⅓ cup (65 g) granulated sugar, plus more as needed

1 teaspoon pure vanilla extract

2 tablespoons water

2 tablespoons cornstarch

Kosher salt

1 box (17 ounces/490 g) frozen vegan puff pastry (2 sheets), thawed overnight in the refrigerator

4 cups (1 L) neutral oil such as vegetable, grapeseed, or avocado, for frying

Combine the coconut strings, coconut milk, sugar, and vanilla in a saucepan and place over medium-high heat. Stir until just combined and bring to a simmer.

Combine the water and cornstarch in a small bowl and stir until smooth. Reduce the heat under the coconut mixture and slowly pour in the slurry, stirring vigorously to prevent clumps. Add a pinch of salt and continue to stir for another minute. Taste the filling and add more sugar to taste. Simmer for another 2 minutes, until sugar has dissolved and the mixture has thickened. Remove from heat and let cool at room temperature for 15 to 20 minutes.

Lay a sheet of puff pastry on a clean work surface. Gently press or roll out the fold, if any. Slice into three 2½- × 7-inch (6 × 18 cm) rectangles using a pizza cutter or a chef's knife and set them aside on a baking sheet without

(continued)

overlapping. Do the same with the second sheet of puff pastry. You should end up with 6 pieces.

Scoop 2 to 3 tablespoons of the filling onto one end of a pastry rectangle, making sure to leave a ½- to 1-inch (1 to 2 cm) border around the edges for sealing the pie. Carefully fold the pastry over the top, covering the filling and making sure the edges are aligned. Gently press the edges together, then use a fork to crimp them and seal the pie. Repeat with the remaining filling and pastry rectangles. (Any leftover coconut filling can be stored in an airtight container for up to 1 week in the refrigerator to use as a topping for pancakes or French toast.)

Fit a wire rack inside a rimmed baking sheet.

Heat the oil in a large heavy-bottomed saucepan over medium-high heat. Dip a wooden chopstick or wooden spoon in the oil to check if it's hot enough. Once the oil bubbles around it, you're ready to fry.

Gently place one or two hand pies in the oil. (Depending on the size of your pan, you may need to work in batches to make sure it is not overcrowded.) Fry the pies on one side for 3 to 4 minutes, until golden brown, then flip using tongs and brown the other side. Use a mesh spider to remove the pies from the oil and transfer them to the wire rack to drain excess oil. Repeat with the remaining pies. Let the pies cool for 5 to 10 minutes before serving.

Store leftover pies in an airtight container in the refrigerator for up to 3 days. Reheat in the air fryer, or in the oven at 350°F (175°C) for 10 minutes.

Peach-Mango Float

If tiramisu had a fruity and tangy cousin, this would be it. Layered with tropical fruits, cream, and graham crackers, this icebox cake is a beginner-friendly masterpiece impressive enough for any special occasion. Canned peach slices shine in this recipe because they're already soaked in a sugar syrup and have a texture similar to a ripe mango, resulting in an even bite. That said, you can also use about 3 to 4 fresh peaches if they're ripe and bursting with juices; peel them first.

SERVES 6 TO 8

1 ripe yellow mango such as Carabao or Ataúlfo

1 can (15 ounces/425 g) peach slices in syrup, drained

2 cups (480 ml) plant-based heavy whipping cream such as Silk or Califia

½ cup (120 ml) sweetened condensed plant-based milk

½ teaspoon pure vanilla extract

About 15 to 20 graham crackers

Cut off the mango cheeks by standing the mango on end and slicing straight down along the seed. Lay each cheek skin side down on a cutting board and carefully scoop the fruit out using a large spoon, making sure to keep the whole cheek intact. Place the flat side down on the cutting board and thinly slice the mango cheek about ⅜ inch (10 mm) thick. Set the slices aside on a dinner plate. Slice the peaches about ⅜ inch (10 mm) thick as well, then set aside on another dinner plate.

Whisk together the whipping cream, condensed milk, and vanilla in a large mixing bowl using an electric hand mixer, for 5 minutes or until stiff peaks form.

Line the bottom of an 8 × 8-inch (20 × 20 cm) square baking dish with an even layer of graham crackers side by side. Break them into pieces to fit the pan as needed.

(continued)

Spread about 2 cups (240 g) of the whipped cream on top of the crackers, making sure to spread it evenly using an offset spatula. Lay down the peach and mango slices on top, alternating and overlapping the fruits when placing them down. Continue layering the whipped cream and fruit slices until you reach the top; finish with the mango and peach slices to create a beautiful fanned look.

Cover the cake with plastic wrap and store it in the refrigerator for at least 6 hours, or overnight for best results.

Let the cake sit at room temperature for 15 minutes before serving on chilled dessert plates.

Store any leftovers in the refrigerator for up to 2 weeks.

NOTE: *If sweetened condensed plant-based milk is too difficult to find, combine ½ cup (100 g) granulated sugar, a pinch of salt, and about 2½ tablespoons of water in a ramekin and microwave for 20 to 30 seconds, until the sugar is completely dissolved. Use this syrup plus an extra ⅓ cup (80 ml) heavy whipping cream to replace the condensed milk.*

Chilled Coconut and Pandan Dessert Salad

BUKO PANDAN

Filipino-style fruit salad is a dessert wonderland in a bowl, filled with a rainbow of sweet and fragrant bits of jellies and toppings. This recipe calls for pandan, a leaf that imparts a strong verdant color and an even stronger flavor similar to vanilla; it is incorporated in two ways. Plant-based stabilizers like agar agar are common in Filipino cooking, vegan or not, making this dessert a convenient crossover between plant-based confections and Filipino cuisine. See the Resources on page 183 for sourcing the pandan leaves and agar agar powder. For the coconut gel, look for Bulacan or Buenas brand nata de coco.

After prepping the jelly, it's as easy as combining all the elements with the coconut cream. Bring this dessert to a potluck or party; it makes enough to serve a gathering.

SERVES 8 TO 10

1 packet (5 ounces/140 g) pandan-flavored agar agar powder

2 pandan leaves

3 cups (720 ml) coconut cream

1 can (11.25 ounces/320 g) sweetened condensed plant-based milk

Pinch of kosher salt

1 cup (150 g) dried sago or mini tapioca pearls

1 bottle (12 ounces/340 g) coconut gel in syrup

2 cups (190 g) frozen coconut meat, thawed

Cook the agar agar following the packet's instructions. Pour it into a 5 × 5-inch (13 × 13 cm) dish or a square container with a lid. Let it cool at room temperature for 30 minutes, then cover and refrigerate for at least 4 hours or overnight.

Tie the pandan leaves into a knot. Combine the coconut cream, condensed milk, salt, and pandan leaves in a saucepan and place over medium-low heat. Stir together until smooth and bring to a gentle simmer until the ingredients are fragrant. Remove from heat and let cool at room temperature for 15 minutes.

Bring another pot of water to a boil over medium-high heat. Add the sago pearls and stir. Cook for 15 minutes or until the pearls are completely translucent. Drain the pearls in a fine-mesh strainer, rinse them in cold water until cool, and set aside in a large mixing bowl.

Slice the agar agar into 1-inch (2.5 cm) chunks and add it to the sago pearls. Drain the liquid from the coconut gel and add the solids to the bowl, along with the coconut meat.

Remove the pandan leaves from the cooled cream mixture and pour over the the sago pearl mixture. Gently mix together until each component is coated and submerged in cream. Cover the bowl with plastic wrap and chill in the refrigerator for at least 2 hours or overnight.

When you're ready to serve, portion the chilled buko pandan into bowls.

Store any leftovers in an airtight container in the refrigerator for up to 1 week, or freeze for up to 2 weeks. Thaw in the refrigerator before serving.

NOTE: *If sweetened condensed plant-based milk is too difficult to find, combine ½ cup (100 g) granulated sugar, a pinch of salt, and about 3 tablespoons of water in a ramekin and microwave for 20 to 30 seconds, until the sugar is completely dissolved. Use this syrup plus an extra ⅓ cup (80 ml) coconut cream to replace the condensed milk.*

Cranberry-Calamansi Fizz

Calamansi is more or less equivalent to a lime in the Philippines. It's a citrus fruit with remarkable tartness and fruitiness that lands somewhere in between oranges, lemons, and a medley of other tropical fruits. It's commonly used as a flavor enhancer in marinades and dipping sauces. When paired with sweet and sour cranberry juice, calamansi makes a deliciously tangy and refreshing beverage. This mocktail is made with sparkling water, but you can spike it with a shot of gin for a little buzz.

SERVES 4 TO 6

CALAMANSI SYRUP

1 cup (200 g) granulated sugar

½ cup (120 ml) water

½ cup (120 ml) calamansi juice or freshly squeezed lime juice

FIZZ

3 cups (720 ml) sparkling water, chilled, plus more as needed

1 cup (240 ml) cranberry juice

6 mint leaves

Ice cubes

Combine the sugar, water, and calamansi juice in a saucepan, stir, and place over medium-low heat. Simmer for 10 minutes or until the sugar has dissolved. Remove from heat, let cool to room temperature, and pour into a clean glass jar.

Mix the sparkling water, cranberry juice, mint, and 3 tablespoons of the calamansi syrup in a large pitcher. Stir to combine. Taste and add more calamansi syrup if you like. Add the ice cubes and stir again before serving.

Store the remaining calamansi syrup tightly capped in the refrigerator for up to a week.

NOTE: *If you can't find straight unsweetened cranberry juice, you can use cranberry juice cocktail and use only half a serving of the calamansi syrup.*

Pineapple Margarita

Pineapple is prized for its sweet and tangy flavor. This cocktail perfectly combines the sweetness of pineapple juice with a zingy, citrusy twist, using silver tequila and fresh lime. It is refreshingly smooth and vibrant, and will transport you to a sun-filled beach vacation.

SERVES 2

3 ounces silver tequila such as Jose Cuervo

3 ounces triple sec

3 ounces pineapple juice

1 cup (240 g) ice cubes, plus more for serving

Kosher salt, for garnish

½ lime, cut into wedges, for serving

Pineapple wedges, for serving (optional)

Combine the tequila, triple sec, pineapple juice, and ice cubes in a cocktail shaker. Cover and shake vigorously for 10 to 15 seconds.

Place a tablespoon of kosher salt on a small plate and flatten it until it's spread evenly. Run a lime wedge around the rims of two cocktail glasses. Press the rim of each glass against the salt to coat.

Fill the glasses with 2 ice cubes each and strain the margarita over the top. To serve, garnish with a lime wedge, and one of pineapple if you like.

Resources

You can find Filipino pantry staples such as sweet chili sauce, and specialty ingredients such as coconut strings (macapuno) or banana leaves, at any Filipino or Asian supermarket.

To find basic items such as soy sauce and cane vinegar in your regular grocery store, check the Asian or international section. Flavor enhancers such as annatto powder and MSG are sold in places like Costco and Walmart. Some Filipino brands to be on the lookout for are Datu Puti, Marca Piña, Mama Sita's, Silver Swan, UFC, Jufran, Buenas, Bulacan, Kapuso, and Jonas.

Of course, you can also purchase items online. In the United States, you can shop for all things Filipino at Sukli (Sukli.com) and Pinoy Groseri (Pinoy-Groseri.com). Asian supermarkets and retailers such as H Mart (HMart.com), Weee! (SayWeee.com), and Just Asian Food (JustAsianFood.com) also carry basic pantry staples. For specific plant-based alternatives, you can shop at Vegan Essentials (VeganEssentials.com). In Canada, you can shop at Sunshine Grocery (SunshineGrocery.ca) or Kabayan Food Mart (KabayanFoodMart.ca).

Here is a list of Filipino basics to keep on hand.

Seasonings

Cane vinegar
Annatto powder

Sauces

Soy sauce
Banana ketchup
Sweet chili sauce

Baking

Ube extract
Ube jam
Coconut strings (macapuno)
Coconut gel in syrup (nata de coco)
Agar agar powder
Glutinous rice flour
Potato starch

Frozen

Grated cassava
Pandan leaves
Banana leaves
Spring roll wrappers
Tofu puffs

Acknowledgments

This book wouldn't be possible without the unconditional support of my mom and dad, who kindly tested recipes and answered my endless questions about Filipino food. Thank you for letting me pursue an unconventional career and encouraging me to keep going. I grew up loving Filipino food because of you, and I'm eternally grateful for your love.

Thank you to my wonderful friends Delaram Basiri, Elliot Sedgwick, Joe Rhodes, Andy Webb, Abi Balingit, Carly McCready, Paul Allardyce, Shadi Basiri, Greg McInnis, Janu Yasotharan, Genesis Fernandez, and Darrel Almario for testing my recipes and giving me insightful notes. To Jynessa Marczuk and Carrie Cai for making me laugh and supporting me when times got rough—you've given me confidence when I needed it most!

To my Filipino family—the Elciarios, Calmas, Salavers, Escanlars, Dalisays, Galvans, Siñels, Esporas, and Ezpeletas in Canada, Japan, and the Philippines, for always being there for me at the right time, even when we're miles apart.

To Lola Didith, for showing me the old fruit trees in the backyard of our ancestral home in Ibajay and teaching me the beauty of tending to a garden and the joy of natural living. Thank you, Lolo Jun, for showing me how important it is to keep laughing as you get older, and my late Lola Nanie, for demonstrating that aging is a wonderful privilege.

Thank you, Auntie Lis, for feeding me different types of kakanin when we visited you and Lola Nanie in Numancia, which inspired some of the recipes in this book, and to Uncle Al for introducing me to the wonderful food of Capiz. To my Tita Nita, for showing me that the sweetest mangoes in the world are found in Igbaras (yes, this is a bold statement and I stand by it). I thought about them when developing the mango desserts in this book.

Thank you, Nina, for telling me about your love for pomelo salad—I wrote my recipe to honor you and Diana.

To my ever so supportive in-laws Janet McKeown, Laurence McKeown, Jake McKeown, Tila Datta, Leah Poole, George Poole, Sam McKeown, and Lydia McKeown for cheering me on and finally adding me to the coveted McKeown group chat.

Thank you to Katherine Cowles, Judy Pray, Mehreen Karim, Suet Chong, Kimberly Ehart, Suzanne Fass, Analucia Zepeda, and everyone else at Workman for your guidance and trusting me to write this book. To the talented photo team, Emma Fishman, Tyna Hoang, Emily Eisen, and Sophie Strangio for bringing my recipes to life and producing the most beautiful images. To Andrea Aliseda and Srishti Jain for the new friendship we've built from our shared experiences writing our first cookbooks. I feel so lucky to have worked with you all.

To Joe—my life partner and best friend. Thank you for testing and tasting all of my recipes, even when they sucked. Thank you for reading every single draft, your patience, the pep talks, and never failing to make me the most perfect cup of Yorkshire tea when I was too tired to function. You see me exactly as I am and make my days shine brighter.

Lastly, to my late grandparents, Andiolina Dalisay Salaver, Andres Siñel Salaver, Rosario Escanlar Elciario, and Ramon Esposas Elciario, who taught me to never forget where I came from. Thank you for showing me resilience and teaching me to love myself and my culture.

Index

D

E

F

G

I

J

K

L

M

N

P

R

S

T

V

W

Ria Elciario-McKeown is a Filipino Canadian writer, recipe developer, and creative producer. At age twelve, Ria and her family moved from Manila to Toronto, which ultimately shaped her unique approach to blending contemporary cooking techniques with traditional Filipino cuisine. Her recipes and articles have been published in media outlets such as Food52, Food Network Canada, and more. When she's not writing about food, Ria covers design and culture for various magazines.